RICHARD GERE

is the man wh[...]e streets of Gree[...]ut whose face an[...]ff that erotic dre[...]

RICHARD GERE

is the dedicated actor who is constantly reaching out for new and different roles to play and shuns the multimillion-dollar-a-movie-star tycoon game.

RICHARD GERE

is the steady love of just one woman, and he refuses to exploit his awesome appeal.

RICHARD GERE

has a superlative "beefcake" physique that is both a natural gift and the result of very hard and demanding work.

RICHARD GERE

can be as testy and unpredictable at times as he is charmingly shy and sensitive at others.

Here are all the faces and facets of Richard Gere—the bad, the good, the great—in a revealing and fascinating close-up of the private man and the public star.

Biography and Autobiography from SIGNET

(0451)

☐ **RICHARD GERE: AN UNAUTHORIZED BIOGRAPHY** by Judith Davis. (126823—$2.95)

☐ **WHERE HAVE I BEEN?** by Sid Caesar with Bill Davidson. (125010—$3.50)*

☐ **TOM SELLECK: AN UNAUTHORIZED BIOGRAPHY** by Jason Bonderoff. (120639—$2.95)*

☐ **ALAN ALDA: AN UNAUTHORIZED BIOGRAPHY** by Jason Bonderoff. (120302—$2.95)

☐ **REPRIEVE** by Agnes de Mille. (119142—$2.95)*

☐ **ELVIS, WHY WON'T THEY LEAVE YOU ALONE?** by May Mann. (118774—$2.95)*

☐ **PENTIMENTO** by Lillian Hellman. (115430—$2.95)

☐ **OFF THE COURT** by Arthur Ashe with Neil Amdur. (117662—$3.50)*

☐ **BITTERSWEET** by Susan Strasberg. (125886—$1.95)*

☐ **SYDNEY POITER: THE LONG JOURNEY (1981 Edition)** by Carolyn H. Ewers. (097327—$1.95)*

☐ **WILMA** by Wilma Rudolph with Bud Greenspan. (099389—$2.25)*

*Price slightly higher in Canada

RICHARD GERE

AN UNAUTHORIZED BIOGRAPHY

by

Judith Davis

A SIGNET BOOK

NEW AMERICAN LIBRARY

TIMES MIRROR

NAL BOOKS ARE AVAILABLE AT QUANTITY DISCOUNTS
WHEN USED TO PROMOTE PRODUCTS OR SERVICES.
FOR INFORMATION PLEASE WRITE TO PREMIUM MARKETING DIVISION,
THE NEW AMERICAN LIBRARY, INC., 1633 BROADWAY,
NEW YORK, NEW YORK 10019.

SIGNET TRADEMARK REG. U.S. PAT. OFF. AND FOREIGN COUNTRIES
REGISTERED TRADEMARK—MARCA REGISTRADA
HECHO EN CHICAGO, U.S.A.

SIGNET, SIGNET CLASSIC, MENTOR, PLUME, MERIDIAN AND NAL BOOKS
are published by The New American Library, Inc.,
1633 Broadway, New York, New York 10019

First Printing, December, 1983

1 2 3 4 5 6 7 8 9

PRINTED IN THE UNITED STATES OF AMERICA

RICHARD GERE

AN UNAUTHORIZED BIOGRAPHY

by
Judith Davis

A SIGNET BOOK
NEW AMERICAN LIBRARY
TIMES MIRROR

Copyright © 1983 by Judith Davis

SIGNET, SIGNET CLASSIC, MENTOR, PLUME, MERIDIAN AND NAL BOOKS
are published by The New American Library, Inc.,
1633 Broadway, New York, New York 10019

First Printing, December, 1983

1   2   3   4   5   6   7   8   9

PRINTED IN THE UNITED STATES OF AMERICA

Contents

Chapter One

Scenes from an Album

Zack Mayo, the new recruit at Officer's Training School in *An Officer and a Gentleman*, collapses facedown on the cement where he has been straining to perform an inhuman number of disciplinary push-ups under the relentless eye of the drill instructor. Suddenly, the whole cocky facade of the man crumbles, and we see the panic of the little boy who is still fighting against the lack of love in his childhood and the insecurity of his outsider's status. It is that defenseless moment that makes the audience take Zack—and actor Richard Gere—to their hearts. Just as they had suspected all along, the sullen stare, that selfish attitude he has been broadcasting were just means of camouflage for the too vulnerable feelings underneath.

RICHARD GERE

*   *   *

Richard Gere decides he would like to spend a few hours of the evening in high style at celebrity-conscious Studio 54 in New York. But when he arrives he is greeted by a swarm of photographers who feast on the faces of the famous. Angrily, he confronts the pushiest of the pack and demands to be left alone. There is suddenly an almost palpable suggestion of violence in his demeanor, and the rest of the photographers crowd nearer in the hope of catching an action-packed moment that will make an even better picture. Just as Gere—his eyes narrowed to slits and his mouth compressed in a straight, tight line—seems ready to explode, a friend intervenes and pulls him almost forcibly away from the photogs and into the club. Minutes later, he is dancing with happy abandon in the periodic flash of the strobe lights, seemingly no longer aware that he is an avidly watched public figure.

Richard Gere paces restlessly around the office of Mike Medavoy, head of Orion Pictures; the room is so big you could do wind sprints in it. He's here to arrive at a decision about starring in *Breathless*, an updated version of Jean-Luc Godard's French classic *A Bout de Soufflé*. He asks pointed questions about the costumes, the sets; he explains at length the qualities he thinks necessary in the actress who will play his leading lady. The assembled executives watch him closely, waiting anxiously for him to make the important decision that will turn all the plans into reality. They have the money, but he has the power; all the good, gray financial managers know that without the charisma of Gere, they have no movie. Suddenly, with a characteristic burst of action, he makes up his mind. He strides across the room and holds out his hand to Jim McBride, the man who initiated the project, co-wrote the script, and will direct the picture. The deal is on!

Jesse Lujack, the small-time hood in big-time trouble in *Breathless*, lies naked in his girl friend's bed, reading her a comic book as she dresses to go out. He rolls over amid the rumpled sheets; he dangles his head off the edge of the bed; he is so engrossed in the exploits of The Silver Surfer that he seems oblivious to all else ... including the presence of the all-seeing camera. Richard Gere makes this nude scene so relaxed, so natural, that it is hard to remember we are an audience and he is an actor playing a very tough assignment. His easy, unselfconscious behavior makes this solo performance one of the film's most intimate moments.

* * *

RICHARD GERE

Richard Gere gets ready to leave his penthouse apartment in New York's Greenwich Village to go out and do some errands. He tucks his faded jeans into the tops of his boots, slips on an old, scarred leather jacket, adds sunglasses and a cap pulled low on his forehead. Out on the street, he is indistinguishable from countless thousands of other Village residents; you would naturally take him for just another young struggling something-or-other—artist, photographer, actor, playwright. While he stands patiently in line to cash a check at the bank, he chats casually with the young woman behind him; she responds warily, with the automatic defenses women have against strange men who try to strike up a conversation. Obviously, she has no idea that she is talking to a celebrity who is the focus of untold numbers of romantic daydreams.

His head shaved, his body looking unexpectedly frail and terribly vulnerable in the striped pajamas that are the uniform of Dachau inmates, a prisoner utters the final, tender, and triumphant words of the play *Bent*: "I love you, I love you." When the curtain falls, the strain of the demanding dramatic role is evident on the face of Richard Gere as he takes a curtain call to a standing ovation. For an actor who lives perilously close to the characters he creates, this long-running, night-after-night immersion in the nightmare of Nazi Germany is an incredibly stressful experience; one that he is unable to shed entirely when he steps off the stage. Friends worry about the effects of this intense involvement, but when the run of the play is completed, his natural resilience enables him to bounce back quickly.

Richard Gere, who ordinarily shuns personal publicity, agrees to make a rare television appearance to help promote his latest picture. He is being interviewed by Gene Shalit on *The Today Show*. As he takes his place on the set, he seems awkward, uncomfortable; he is obviously not used to the whole impersonal, exploitive celebrity-chewing machine, and his unease is projected vividly on the video screen. Later he remarks, "I didn't know why I was there and what I was supposed to be doing." Thereafter, he makes a practice of rigorously avoiding all of the sex-symbol publicity that the media are all too anxious to confer upon him.

Richard Gere is hard at work getting ready for his role in the new film, *Cotton Club*, in which he plays a jazz musician turned nightclub owner. It's a good chance for him to display the wide range of his musical talent, and he is determined to be at his best. He practices seriously for hours every day, on the trumpet, the piano, and the guitar, so the rare scenes in which he plays an instrument will look and sound right. Few performers are so conscientious, so determined to make even the minor facets of a screen characterization seem realistic and believable. "I've never known any actor except Dustin Hoffman to give so much attention to every detail," says the film's producer/director, Robert Evans. "But Dustin does it for his character; Richard does it because he cares about the whole movie."

These scenes reflect some of the many facets of Richard Gere, the complex human being who has suddenly become one of the biggest box-office draws in Hollywood. Let's look at some of the contradictions. . . .

Richard Gere has undeniably worked hard to achieve his success. He's paid his dues with years of struggle to express himself as an actor, and it's obvious that he enjoys the position and the leverage he has, now that he has joined the ranks of the bankable male stars, one of the handful of actors whose mere presence in a film is enough to make studio heads whip out their checkbooks and clamor to supply financial backing. Yet at the same time, he is wary of the traps such great success can create. Instinctively, he rejects the usual accessories of superstardom—the eternally waiting limo, the luxurious mansion in Beverly Hills, the omnipresent entourage of hangers-on who exist to tell a star exactly what he wants to hear: "You'll be great in that role, babe, would I lie to you?"

Then there are his complex feelings about his status as a sex symbol. There are fans who see Richard Gere simply as so many pounds of male flesh on the hoof, two-dimensional beefcake to put on the wall right next to the poster of Rick Springfield, under the soft-focus photo of a white stallion standing in a field of wild flowers. But the man himself fights against fitting neatly into any category. "It's flattering to be desired," he told a reporter, "flattering that people accept the reality of the characters I play. But in the end, the characters that are given life through me have an existence of their own, and I take no responsibility for them outside of their artistic context. It's ridiculous to assume that because I play a gigolo or any other character onscreen, I must play the same role offscreen. I'm an actor. I refuse to give up who I am because of what people expect me to be."

But it's not always easy to separate the actor from the person. After all, they inhabit the same body. And it's a body that Richard Gere works hard to keep in the best possible condition. He works out with weights and does the kind of exercises that make you hot and sweaty and almost light-headed with fatigue. He has earned that body that is both an actor's tool and a fan's delight, and it is clear that he is comfortable with it; you can't fake that kind of unselfconscious display. When he peels off his shirt, it almost seems to be an act of generosity, a willingness to share with the audience, a secret signal to his fans that he understands their daydreams.

But although he is perfectly willing to bare his body, he refuses to do the same with his soul. He is resolutely private, determined to keep his daily life and his inner thoughts to himself. He rarely gives interviews, and when he does, his responses to questions are guarded and defensive. He has been accused of being antagonistic to the press whenever they try to push beyond the limits of his screen appearances and acting performances. Although he has given some long and illuminating interviews concerning the nature of his craft as an actor, he can be visibly annoyed when an interviewer persists in returning the conversation again and again to the subject of sex symbols. It is an index to the ferocity of his desire for privacy that no journalist has ever seen the inside of his apartment; he fears that on his home turf, they might be able to pick up tiny clues that could lead them to the real Richard Gere.

Scenes from an Album

Whoever the real Richard Gere is, you can bet that the public will never have access to him. The private man hides behind the public body.

Chapter Two

In the Beginning

Richard Gere is currently riding the crest of the wave. He first attracted the attention of movie audiences and critics in his supporting role in *Looking For Mr. Goodbar*, alternately threatening Diane Keaton and sending her into ecstasy. In 1980 came the release of *American Gigolo*, which grossed $9 million at the box office in its first two weeks. Gere was suddenly "hot" in the film industry. At the same time, he was receiving the first unanimously favorable reviews of his career, for his performance in *Bent* on Broadway; that gave him another boost on the ladder to stardom. The year of the big breakthrough was 1982, with *An Officer and a Gentleman* broadening his appeal to the mass movie audience. That film made more than $100 mil-

lion in the first six months of its release. Only
E.T. did better at the box office that year.

When that kind of money talks, Hollywood
listens. Richard Gere was suddenly on the
receiving end of a flood of propositions; as he
commented cynically, "There are lots of offers
when they figure they can make money off
you." Inevitably, many of those offers were for
the same kind of sexy parts he had played in
his earlier films. But Gere had other ideas about
the way he wanted his career to develop. "I
certainly could have played characters that focus on sex and booked myself up for the next
ten years for an enormous amount of money.
I've consciously not done that. I've chosen roles
that allow me to explore things I haven't done
before."

His recent choice of roles suggests something
of his breadth as an actor. First came *Breathless*,
which he was drawn to because of his respect
for the original Godard film. He plays a character who is a born loser, possessed of a certain
amount of animal cunning but almost no intel-
ligence—Gere calls him a real bozo. Next was
Beyond the Limit, based on an ironic tale by
Graham Greene about South American guerrillas
kidnapping a man they assume to be a high
government official who in reality is a nobody.
Gere plays a confederate of the revolution-
aries, a character who is trying to find a way to
make a silk purse out of the sow's ear he dis-

covers they have snatched. Following that will be *Cotton Club*, in which he plays a failed musician turned nightclub boss. Each of these characters draws on different facets of Richard Gere's performing ability, and none of them limits him to the confines of simply being displayed as a sex symbol.

The fact that Richard Gere has been offered so many challenging roles is one yardstick of his success. Another, of course, is the money he makes through his screen appearances. For *American Gigolo*, he was paid $350,000, making him an incredible bargain compared with the film's earnings. But times have changed: his salary for *Cotton Club* is reported to be a cool $1,600,000! And the chances are he could easily make twice that much for the next film he signs to do. Not bad for an actor whose first featured performance in a film came only a few years ago, in 1977.

How did Richard Gere come so far, so fast?

He wasn't the kind of kid you would have picked out as a future superstar. He was born in Philadelphia on August 29, 1950, but his family moved to a farm on the outskirts of Syracuse, New York, when he was still very young. Syracuse was, and is, a remarkably pleasant city, still quite open and green, with a total population of more than 600,000 people in its greater metropolitan area. Syracuse University and its 20,000 students are an important influence on the life of the city; there is a symphony orchestra, two excellent museums, a theater showing the latest European films. Most of the residents work at some kind of manufacturing concern: General Electric, Carrier, Allied Chemical are there, along with a couple of large breweries. But there is still open farmland nearby, and the shores of Lake Ontario are less than an hour's drive away. All in all, a good place to grow up.

Richard was one of five children who were raised in comfortable middle-class surroundings. Richard's father, Homer Gere, soon gave up farming and became a hardworking insurance salesman. Richard explains, "He's not one of those huckster types. He's really great at it because he believes in it. He's like a minister; he really wants to help people, and they love him." The Gere family life seems to have been warm and supportive, and Richard has described his parents as "sweet, honest, straight, churchgoing people." All of the kids shared an interest in music (Richard's brother now performs as a concert pianist) and Richard says that even now, "When I go home, we all play together, then switch instruments and play something else." He and his older sister Susan used to entertain the family after dinner with their imitations. "She would do an imitation of Edie Adams doing an imitation of Marilyn Monroe," Gere recollected recently. "I would do Ernie Kovacs or those characters from the Steve Allen show." Susan kids him that she remembers him "brooding at the age of two," but he takes the joke in good part. He remains close to his family and seldom misses a Christmas at home.

Richard himself was a talented musician. His original instrument was the trumpet, and by the time he was fourteen, he was playing in public and had organized a small band to play at weddings and other social gatherings. Two years later, he was the guest soloist for the Syracuse Symphony for a performance of Handel's *Messiah*. In his teens, he also learned to play guitar, piano, banjo, and sitar. "I convinced myself I could play ragas, but it was a joke." It was music that led him to the theater. He started writing background music for school productions and eventually decided he'd like to try acting in them as well; he had no trouble winning leading roles. Soon he became so interested in acting that once he decided to run away so he could go to New York's off-Broadway theaters. Having prudently purchased a roundtrip ticket so he could get home again, he was free to wander around Greenwich Village, seeing one play after another until his money ran out.

The arts were not his only extracurricular activity. He was also an excellent gymnast who competed on the school team, and even then he devoted a lot of time to keeping his body in shape. He joined the Boy Scouts. He liked to go out and have a good time. Unfortunately, all of these enthusiasm left him scant time for his studies, and his grades reflected that fact.

Richard Gere graduated from high school in 1967, and in many ways, he was a child of his time. He has said that he remembers feeling "pretty confused"; many other young people shared that feeling of confusion as the nation entered a period of rapid social change. The National Organization of Women had just been founded by feminists who were derisively called "bra burners." Blacks, too, were ready for change; there were frightening and destructive riots in poor black communities in Newark and Detroit, despite the nonviolence urged by the soon-to-be-assassinated Martin Luther King, Jr. Students protested the policies of their schools and universities, and when we all began to understand the true scope of the war in Vietnam, the protests escalated in frequency and intensity. President Johnson, a target of growing opposition, was soon to give up the hope of another term in office. John Wayne began to make a movie glorifying the Green Berets, while rock idol Jim Morrison, wearing obscenely tight black leather pants, sang ominously about the Unknown Soldier. Soon a whole generation of teenagers brought up on the hard beat and tough images of rock would convene at Woodstock.

This was the social background of Richard Gere's coming of age. He describes himself at this time as having his head "full of punks, motorcycles, leather jackets, knives, violence—the whole James Dean–Brando bit." He decided that his future lay in the performing arts, either music or the theater. His father was dismayed by his decision and urged him instead to do "something constructive." Richard comments sympathetically, "I didn't understand his fears, thought they were bourgeois. But he knew I'd have to go through hell and he just didn't want to see it. I went through a young-man-paranoid stage. I was dead middle-class, and I felt I had to do something special. I didn't want what I thought was that amorphous middle-class nowhere status. Even though my parents questioned what I was doing, they were loving, sweet, and supportive. But they had no frame of reference for understanding what I was going through."

Despite a certain taste for the role of the rebel, Gere's first step away from home was conventional enough: He decided to go to college. He was accepted at the University of Massachusetts, in Amherst, largely as a result of his qualifications as a gymnast, since his grades were not particularly impressive. During his two years on the campus, he kept up with his athletics and played occasional gigs in local nightspots. He had leading roles in several college dramatic productions. "I was doing Pinter plays all the time, and it was a liberating experience. I suppose that's the initial rush about acting, that you can get outside yourself and become another jerk you're not responsible for." He chose to major in philosophy, and later explained his choice: "There were all those questions I couldn't answer. I kept asking why, why, why? But the answers I got from courses in logic and meaning seemed to lead to proving I didn't exist. Those two years at college seem to me now as a destructive experience." What he remembers most clearly about that experience is that he virtually submerged himself in movies. "I had no real friends, and I suppose that was why I went on a movie kick. I remember walking back at two in the morning, night after night, after six hours at the movies." He soaked up films by Bergman, Antonioni, Bresson; he learned to recognize and respect the skills of a great director.

The summer after his sophomore year at U. Mass, Gere agreed, for a lark, to go along with a friend who wanted to audition for the company of the Provincetown Playhouse, a Cape Cod summer theater renowned for the quality of its productions. Although Richard was just along for the ride, once they got there he decided—what the hell—he might as well audition himself. The director at the time, Bill Roberts, still remembers that occasion. "Here was this student who's never had his hair cut—torn blue jeans, leather jacket, the hippie bit—who read brilliantly. He seemed quite indifferent. But when I had posted the cast list with his name on it, I looked out the window and saw Richard run down the beach and hurl himself into the sea." Ironically, the friend he had accompanied didn't make the list.

That summer in Provincetown was a good one. The repertory company (which paid him $28.70 a week) was set up to do a new play every two weeks. That meant he was acting in one play every night while rehearsing the next in the daytime. Among the productions he would be appearing in were *The Great God Brown*, Tennessee Williams's *Camino Real*, *The Collection*, and *Rosencrantz and Guildenstern are Dead*. "I played the leads. Why they let me, I don't know." In the relaxed atmosphere of this summer gathering place for artists, writers, and intellectuals, he made friends with director Roberts and his wife Janet, a New York literary agent. At the end of the season, Bill Roberts made a suggestion. He was going out to Seattle for a season as the designer with the Seattle Repertory Company. How would Gere like to come along?

It didn't take Richard long to say yes. "College wasn't for me. I knew I didn't want to be told what to do anymore." For him, as for many other bright young people in the late sixties, college seemed irrelevant: at best a waste of time and at worst a mutilation of one's creative faculties. At that time, he was probably more committed to the notion of leaving college than he was to a career in the theater. "I wasn't yet sure if acting was the career I wanted, but I guess I had to be leaning that way if I went through with learning and performing all those parts." So he quit school and headed west.

Life in Seattle turned out to be unexpectedly tough. He earned only $75 a week from the repertory company, and even in 1970 that wasn't enough to live on and still have anything left over for an occasional beer and some movie tickets. One survival strategy was playing the piano for background music at fashion shows— anything to make a little extra money.

It might all have been worth it if he'd been happy with the repertory theater. But he found the atmosphere too institutional, too much like school, which he thought he'd left behind. They did a new production every month, and Richard had the leading role in *Volpone*, for which he also composed some incidental music. But somehow he didn't catch fire, and he no longer won all the leading roles. He began to question his commitment to the theater. Maybe he wasn't cut out to be an actor after all. . . .

The upshot was that in the summer of 1970, he bought a used Econoline van, invested in a new muffler, and drove it back east. He ended up in Vermont, camping out on a 300-acre farm idyllically situated on the top of a mountain, complete with trout streams and view. He got in touch with some of the guys he had played with in high school and college, and brought them together to form a rock band. For six weeks, they practiced amid the pastures of rural Vermont. He played bass and guitar and sang rather in the style of Van Morrison. The entire episode sounds like something out of an Ann Beattie short story: good friends living a communal lifestyle in a back-to-nature setting and devoting themselves to creativity. Unfortunately, the ending of the story has the Beattie quality of disillusionment. Six weeks was all it took for the group to realize they didn't like each other and couldn't get along together. (Gere remembers that they had rather appropriately chosen the name The Strangers.) The sixties dream abruptly foundered on reality.

For Richard, the question was where to go next. Surely not back to school: That period of his life was conclusively over. And although his parents remained loving and supportive, he knew he couldn't go home again.

Well, what about New York? He remembered those happy hours spent in the little off-Broadway theaters. Maybe he did want to go on acting after all; he just didn't want to do it in Seattle. But in New York, it could all be different. Challenging roles to try for, a committed theatrical community to be a part of, the big exciting city as a background for it all.

"One day I decided, okay, I'm going to New York and get real serious about acting."

Chapter Three

Paying Some Dues

Like countless thousands of other young performers, Richard Gere decided to test his talent and his commitment in the crucible of New York. Sure, he knew he was taking a gamble, but after all, talent will take you a long way. . . . Paul Newman and Montgomery Clift found stardom that way, didn't they? What's so unreasonable about hoping that history will repeat itself? Besides, Richard could comfort himself with the fatalistic attitude he had absorbed from reading about the beliefs of Eastern religions: "Things happen as they happen, as they *have* to happen. They could happen no other way." His way was to go to New York.

One of the tricks life plays on all of us is to make us believe that our own actions and decisions are unique expressions of our individuality; it is not until years later that we can look back and see that in fact we have behaved just like a lot of other people in our age group and situation. It may well have seemed to the twenty-one-year-old Richard Gere that he was making a dramatic break with tradition when he made the move to New York instead of to Hollywood. But, to the contrary, he was simply entering a time-honored tradition of the performing life.

The familiar drama begins with the first-act decision to take the big city by storm. But the script decrees that in the second act, expectations will be confounded. New York turns out to be expensive, hostile, incredibly competitive. Hundreds of talented actors are forced to practice their craft only by listing the daily specials for patrons of the restaurant where they wait tables. They live in tiny apartments in dangerous neighborhoods. By the time they have invested in new glossies to hand out, and transportation money to innumerable fruitless auditions, they have spent their food budget for the week; so they cadge leftovers from the restaurant and accept all invitations that include free food and drink. Of course, sooner or later, they do get a part. But the play closes in two days. Or the critics never mention them by name. Or the production is performed in a theater with a capacity of 100 seats that is never more than half full, largely with friends and relatives of people connected with the enterprise. A few of these experiences make being rejected in auditions seem like a desirable shortcut to obscurity.

In most cases, the third act follows a similarly rigid pattern. If the drama is to have a warmly satisfactory ending, the performer learns to relinquish the unreasonable dream of stardom and settle instead for ordinary rewards of life: a happy marriage, a decent job, maybe the chance to teach drama in a good high school. Or, if the ending is to be tragic, we see the aging hopeful wasting yet another year of precious life chasing the phantom of success, as looks fade along with the resumé.

What is exceptional about Richard Gere is that he was able to rewrite the script for the third act, to turn it into a triumphant conclusion in which true talent is recognized and a star is born. Such an ending happens only a few times in every decade. Of course, it takes more than just talent, or luck, to succeed where so many people have failed. Richard attributes his success to focus. "I knew people who were as talented as I was who didn't have it. I think I've always felt that it was focus and commitment and concentration that made the thing happen. When things fuck up, you just keep going. Most people give in and say, 'Fuck it, I'm not cut out for this,' and they do something else. You've got to outlast all the fuck-ups and just keep going, keep going, keep going."

Gere's commitment to "keep going" was immediately apparent. The very day he arrived in New York, he started looking for work as an actor. His initial step was to visit Janet Roberts, the wife of his first theatrical mentor. She helped out by sending him around to see one of her friends, Ed Limato, then a theatrical agent with International Creative Management, one of the biggest and most powerful agencies in the business. Ed, who is still Gere's primary agent, was one of the first in a series of professionals who recognized Richard's potential for a successful career as an actor, and lent a helping hand. Ed has no difficulty remembering their first meeting. "I signed him without ever seeing him work. He was a different-looking guy at the time, another long-hair rebel with a guitar. But you could see in him the quality of a leading man: handsome, with an element of danger to him, and unpredictability."

It didn't take Limato long to find a role for his multitalented client. He got Richard a part in an off-Broadway production called *Soon*, a "rock opera" no doubt seeking to imitate the recent success of *Hair*. Richard was not only slated to act, he also composed some of the music and played several instruments on stage: he reminisces: "Played bass, slide guitar, guitar. Played more instruments than the entire band, and was making less money than anyone else." Onstage, he was certainly in good company.

Other actors in *Soon* included Peter Allen, Barry Bostwick, and Nell Carter. The musical opened one night in January, 1971, and closed the following night. It was to be the first in a series of near misses that would test severely Gere's determination to succeed.

There was no immediate theatrical work in sight, but Richard Gere had to live *somewhere*, so he moved into a very small apartment in a very undesirable section of the East Village. He later described it to Rex Reed as a place where "they don't deliver mail, and the Fire Department doesn't even answer an alarm." The only good thing about being unemployed was that it gave him the opportunity to frequent the many movie houses that specialized in foreign films; he learned to admire the work of Fassbinder, Wenders, and Herzog. He was also a frequent visitor at the classes of the American Ballet Theatre, watching the way the dancers moved and conveyed emotion through the use of the body alone. He recalls those early months: "It was a painful time but romantic at the same time." In a less ebullient moment, he recalled more of the dark side of the early struggles: "It took me two years just to get used to New York. Every day I found myself on the railing of the East River trying not to jump in. I came here knowing nobody. The only person I knew in New York was an old girl friend who didn't want to know I was alive."

But Gere stuck to the search for work as an actor, despite the low-rent lifestyle it imposed. And eventually he landed another role. The production was another mix of music and drama, called *Richard Fariña: A Long Time Coming and a Long Time Gone.* Fariña was something of a cult hero of the sixties. A talented musician, he made several albums that featured evocative lyrics often darkened by images of death and emotional loss, an original sound that combined guitar and dulcimer (Fariña's instrument) and close vocal harmonies between himself and his wife/partner Mimi, the sister of Joan Baez. In addition to his songs, Fariña wrote poetry and also completed a novel, *Been Down so Long it Looks Like Up to Me,* which was praised by both *The New York Times* and Thomas Pynchon. It was perhaps an integral part of his legend that he was killed in a motorcycle accident in April, 1966, while returning home from a party celebrating the publication of that novel.

Gere was cast in the leading role of Fariña by director Robert Greenwood, who had also been the director of the short-lived *Soon.* He remembers what it was like to work with Richard Gere in those early days: "Gere had enormous energy. He never stopped working. If a rehearsal was supposed to go eight hours, Gere would go twelve. There was no doubt in my mind he would become a star." The role of Richard Fariña was obviously one that Richard Gere could identify with; unfortunately, the audiences in late 1971 were more resistant to the subject matter. Gere soon had his second experience of a play folding quickly under him. Perhaps the best thing to come out of the whole experience was his meeting with a young actress named Penelope Milford. It was the start of a long and intimate relationship that was to mean much to both of them.

Meanwhile, Richard was once again looking for work. Parts were hard to find, and most of the time he paid the rent with his unemployment check. He says, "I can't remember much about those days, except that I was going through my young-man-paranoid phase, when obviously the universe was against me. But I actually got more work than most young actors get, though there was a spell when I didn't work for a whole year. I had only one outside job in all that time. I was a dishwasher at Hungry Charlie's down in Greenwich Village for two weeks. I was too embarrassed to wait tables, because people would see me and know I was doing it for the money. Besides, back there by myself with the dishes and the steam, I could think. No one was bugging me or hounding me, because no one else wanted to do that job."

He once said of this period: "Wrist-slitting time in Manhattan." Perhaps that sense of discouragement explains why he decided that a change of scene would help him keep going. In 1972, he went to London.

His first break in London came from the British company of *Grease*, the Broadway hit that offered audiences a nostalgic look back at the style of the fifties. He was cast in the macho role of Danny Zuko, the leader of a teen street gang (the role was originated in the American production by his *Soon* co-star, Barry Bostwick). It was a good piece of casting; Gere was able to suggest the hot personality that lurked under the cool style Danny affected. His success with that role led to an invitation to do a season of repertory with England's prestigious Young Vic, traditionally a proving ground for that country's talented young actors. That season provided good training for Gere.

He returned to New York as a cast member in the Young Vic production of *The Taming of the Shrew*, performed at the Brooklyn Academy of Music. He played the part of Christopher Sly, the drunken victim of a practical joke in the two-scene prologue that sets up the story of Petruchio and Katherina. Several reviewers took the time and trouble to commend the performance of the single American member of the cast; he was called "funny and imaginative."

Back home, Richard Gere settled into a new apartment, a converted storefront in the West Village, not far from the raunchy strip of gay bars in the shadow of the West Side Highway.

"It was a plumber's store before I moved in. It's the size of one of those Puerto Rican groceries, ten feet wide and about twenty feet long and divided into three rooms with two lofts and a fireplace. It's a gas. The problem is, there's no light. No sunlight. I have a big window on the street filled with plants. It's terrific after midnight." That was the time the teenage hoods came around to beat up the gays patronizing bars in the neighborhood. Richard Gere was once the victim of some of these real-life punks, the seventies version of Danny Zuko and his gang. "They probably thought I was gay because I had on a leather jacket and motorcycle boots. I've always worn that. I've been into motorcycles for years."

Somehow, after Richard Gere returned from London, things seemed to get just a little bit easier . . . perhaps because insiders were already beginning to recognize him as one of the most promising young actors of the decade. He got a chance to appear on Broadway for some months as Barry Bostwick's replacement in the long-running *Grease*. He had a bit part in an episode of the TV series *Kojak*; at that time, one of the few shows to be taped in New York, *Kojak* offered paychecks and visibility to many aspiring, young theatrical talents. He later appeared in a made-for-TV movie called *Strike*, and also got to speak the single word, "hello," on a Marlo Thomas special.

Paying Some Dues

More significant recognition came when Judy Lamb, a casting agent for Joseph Papp's Public Theater, who had seen Gere in *Soon*, chose Richard for one of Papp's Shakespearean productions. Gere got the part of Demetrius, a confused mortal who falls victim to the fairy spells of Oberon and Puck in *A Midsummer Night's Dream*. It was performed at Lincoln Center, and Gere acquitted himself creditably.

But the real turning point in these early years of struggle came in the spring of 1975, when Richard Gere was selected to play the leading role—in fact, the *only* role—in an off-off-Broadway production of a one-act play written by Sam Shepard. It was called *Killer's Head*, and it basically amounted to one long monologue delivered by Mazon, a convicted murderer. He talks about his fantasy plans for the nonexistent future as he sits on the stage strapped into an electric chair with a blindfold over his eyes. It's difficult to imagine a more demanding part; *Killer's Head* is hard on both the audience and the star. Gere called it a "bizarre" play, but he went on to say, "It was the first part in which I felt I really connected. As a prisoner strapped to an electric chair and blindfolded, I couldn't move my body, and so it had to be a total manifestation of energy. No narcissism, no wondering how I looked." Although Shepard is now recognized as one of America's most talented and innovative young playwrights, *Killer's*

Head never attracted a large crowd, and it didn't run very long. But some critics made a point of seeing the play, and they were unanimous in praising Gere's performance. One said he was "remarkable in the few exciting moments we had with him," and another said that he performed "the garrulous, streaming consciousness patter with great virtuosity."

Perhaps the praise that meant the most to Gere came from Wynn Handman, the director of the American Place Theatre, where the play was performed. To help the young actor cope with such a technically demanding role, Handman gave him some additional coaching; it was the one and only experience Richard had trying to learn the business of acting from someone else, and in later years he spoke appreciatively of Handman's help. Among Handman's other students have been such stars as Frank Langella, Joel Grey, and James Caan, but he is most outspoken in his praise of Gere. "He is serious, a devoted actor and an adventurous one. Richard is talented. He goes very deeply into character. He was spectacularly good in the Sam Shepard play, *Killer's Head*, which is just a long monologue. While strapped into an electric chair, he had to hold the audience with just his facial expressions and the rhythmic cadence of his language."

Although *Killer's Head* closed fairly quickly, Gere's success with the unusual role led to more offers of work. Over the summer, he shot his first movie, *Report to the Commissioner*, which was a seamy cops-and-robbers melodrama about the gradual corruption of an idealistic young rookie. The leading role was played by Michael Moriarty, and the film was produced by Mike Frankovich and directed by Milton Katselas. Gere's small part, which he later said he did "for the bucks" was that of Billy, a street-smart pimp. The movie's lack of both critical acclaim and box-office success makes it difficult for Gere fans to catch his screen performance debut. But if you had happened to be one of the few who saw the flick when it was released, you might have noticed an actor who brought an unusual degree of intensity to his small and insignificant part.

Gere's first taste of movie acting left him eager to return to the stage. "There are layers of energy between the people on stage and in the audience," he told an interviewer. "There's a dual effect, depending on how much energy you give. It's riveting to know that something might go wrong." But nothing did go wrong in his next theatrical vehicle, an American version of a successful British farce, called *Habeas Corpus*. It opened on Broadway in the fall of 1975, with Gere playing the role of Mr. Shanks, a traveling salesman for a company that makes falsies. As you might guess from the mere description of this one role, the jokes in the play all revolved around sex. Perhaps that's why it ran for three and a half months and gave Richard Gere a chance to stop visiting his local unemployment office for a while. *Habeas Corpus* was written by Alan Bennett, directed by Frank Dunlop and starred Rachel Roberts. The reviews were as good as anyone could have expected for such a frothy creation.

As soon as that production closed, Richard Gere was offered another role. It was in a revival of Clifford Odets's play *Awake and Sing*, being mounted by the prestigious McCarter Theater in Princeton, New Jersey. The play was first produced on Broadway in 1935, and the timely subject was the effort of an ordinary New York Jewish family to fight for survival during the Depression. Gere's role of Ralph, the ambitious young son who longs for better days, was originated by John Garfield; an interesting coincidence, since once Richard Gere became a star, more than one critic compared his tough-but-tender appeal to that of Garfield. The producer created another link with the original production when he signed Morris Carnovsky to recreate his role of Grandpa. Gere appreciated the chance to work with such a skillful veteran. "A lot of actors have lost touch with that," he commented in an interview. "There should be continuity in the theater." He went on to explore some of his reasons for concentrating on the stage during the early years of his career. "In the theater, you don't build a persona the way you do in the movies. You make no money. You don't get your name in the papers. You play characters. The pleasure lies in the work—the learning, learning, learning." Apparently he was making the most of his learning opportunities, for his work in *Awake and Sing* won him excellent reviews. Clive Barnes, in *The New York Times*, commented favorably on his ability to project a sense of "controlled anguish."

But Richard Gere would not appear on the stage again for more than four years. His career took a significant turn as Hollywood beckoned. His second film appearance, another small part, had a lot to do with it. In 1976, he was cast in director John Hancock's World War II drama, *Baby Blue Marine*. Gere played the part of a shell-shocked young Marine raider whose war experiences had turned him into a psychopathic menace. As it was written, it was clear that his part was largely a device to set the plot in motion. He meets the hero, played by Jan-Michael Vincent, gains his confidence, then knocks him out and trades uniforms with him, thereby launching him on the series of adventures that are the main elements of the plot. But in Gere's hands, the small part came alive and turned into something memorable, a full-scale portrayal of a wartime tragedy. (One unusual aspect of this appearance was that the character was supposed to be an albino, so Richard played the part as a blond . . . an unsettling, almost ghostly version of someone we have learned to identify as darkly handsome.)

The movie was not a success, but Gere's performance impressed Hollywood insiders. And the strength of that performance was what casting director Judy Lamb, by that time working for Paramount Pictures, used to get Richard his next film role.

Stardom was just around the corner.

Chapter Four
The First Major Film

New Year's Day, 1977. If Richard Gere had sat down to think about his past and speculate on his future, would he have been optimistic or discouraged? He had spent seven years trying to build a career as an actor. There were people—and important people, too—who already recognized that he was an unusual talent. He'd won some good roles, certainly more than most other struggling young performers, and he had a slim sheaf of appreciative reviews of his work. He'd had the chance to play in works by Shakespeare, Tennessee Williams, Clifford Odets, Tom Stoppard, Sam Shepard, and each role had taught him a little something new about acting and about himself. Unlike many other aspiring stars, he had been able to survive, and even to grow, in the fierce competition of New York. And he had learned to live in that tough city—no more thoughts of jumping into the East River. He felt at home there, comfortable in his funny storefront apartment. He even sustained a good relationship with the lady in his life, Penelope Milford, who appreciated him as an actor as well as a man, and who helped him keep his feet on the ground and his courage up for the next challenge. Such things are not negligible accomplishments in life.

On the other hand, major success had so far eluded him. If you added up all the people who had seen him perform on the stage in any role whatever, it wouldn't come to a very large total. People connected with the theater might recognize his name, but for the general public, it was still "Richard who?" His two screen appearances had attracted little attention; his parts were simply too small, and the vehicles themselves too undistinguished. A good index of the state of his career was that despite all his credits, he still found that most months he had to pay the rent with his unemployment check.

But early in 1977, events began to set in motion a change. Judy Lamb brought Richard to the attention of others at Paramount. In particular, she commended him to director Terence Malick, who had signed with Paramount for his second film. Hollywood considered Malick a hot young talent because of the unexpected success of his first film, *Badlands* (1973). It was an unusual combination of romanticism and realism, focusing on the story of a teenage couple on the run from the law for committing a string of murders. The movie was a critical success that displayed surprising strength at the box office.

Now Malick had signed to make a second film, which was to become *Days of Heaven*, and he had sketched out a screenplay set in 1916, of young urban factory workers who head west to find work as migrant field laborers. But Malick had not yet cast any of the major roles. He wanted to avoid, if possible, using big stars who would bring a well-known persona of their own to the film, but he was even more concerned about finding exactly the right actor for each role. For the male lead, he was considering John Travolta, who had just starred in the hit *Saturday Night Fever*. There was the objection that he was too well known, but on the other hand he had the intensity the part called for. Then Judy Lamb told Malick about Richard Gere, and the focus of his deliberation shifted. Gere explained, "Terence Malick knew me by reputation. He got in touch. We talked a lot and we did a lot of things on tape. He tried to match up actors. There was no screen test, per se. Genevieve Bujold had been set for the female lead but backed out, for her own personal reasons." In fact, it took nearly three months, and countless interviews and conversations, before Malick and producer Jacob Brackman made up their minds: They would go with Gere. The also-ran Travolta had to be content with starring in *Grease!*

The rest of the cast was more quickly assembled. Playwright Sam Shepard, in his first shot at acting, was signed to play the part of a wealthy farmer; Brooke Adams, a TV actress, was cast as Gere's girl friend; and eleven-year-old Linda Manz got the part of the hero's younger sister. Just as important to the finished film as Malick's choice of actors was his decision to use Nestor Almendros as the cinematographer. Almendros had shot films for François Truffaut and, more recently, the critically acclaimed *Claire's Knee* for Eric Rohmer. The hallmark of Almendros's work is its great beauty. It gave Malick a way to see the story and to express its emotions. (Some critics felt the choice of Almendros was Malick's undoing; Stanley Kauffmann, movie critic for *The New Republic,* remarked unkindly, "Malick has proven, by doing this, the last thing he wanted to prove: There is no such thing as an artist-cinematographer; there are only good cinematographers who sometimes work for artists.")

Most of the picture was shot on location. Malick chose the Canadian prairies, which for some reason directors all seem to think looks more like the American heartland than any place actually in the United States. (The Canadian prairies were also chosen as the location for Superman's All-American boyhood home.) Richard Gere remembers, "The original shooting took three months, and we filmed in Lethbridge, Alberta, near Calgary. By the time we left, we were all crazed. Everyone was manic." Part of the reason, no doubt, was the remoteness of the place where they were working; it is common for actors on location to get a kind of cabin fever. But part of the reason was also Malick's peculiar way of working, which put a special strain on his actors.

Malick began shooting with a script, about a love triangle, but he intended the plot to be only a starting point from which the true film would emerge. Time and time again, he became dissatisfied with what he had on paper and asked his actors to think of something better. According to Gere, "Malick despises his own writing, so we'd be shooting a major scene, say, in a wheat field, and he'd stop us and say, 'This is bullshit—do something else.' We improvised plenty. . . ." He told another interviewer, "It was not an easy process working with Terry. The movie that was shot was not the script I had read. It kept changing. Terry's a poet, and vague about what he wants. We'd set up for a scene and Terry would say, 'It's—it's like the wind coming through the window.' And I'd say, 'Okay, I've got it.' We'd do take after take, and a three-page scene might finally wind down to two or three lines. What he wanted was a moment of truth, and you can't tell anyone what truth is and how to get it." And in a more thoughtful interview for *Film Comment*, about the directors he had worked with, Gere added, "Terry didn't really know about actors, so it was a question of not knowing quite how they work, not knowing how to communicate with them. He knows when it's right; he knows when it's wrong; but he doesn't quite know how to make it work or why it's wrong. . . . He doesn't really care about the dramaturgy; he wanted a very special thing, a breath of life, something very difficult to communicate."

These problems were especially tough for so dedicated an actor as Richard Gere, and the fact that *Days of Heaven* was his first major film made it all the more nerve-wracking. But despite the obvious problems, Richard remains vocal in his appreciation of Malick's talent. "Terry is a very cerebral and sensitive director," he says, and he goes on to call the man a genius. And he would definitely like to do another film with him sometime in the future: "I'd like to work with Terry again. I mean, after what we've both been through, I think we could work a lot better together."

Critical opinion is somewhat divided as to the success of *Days of Heaven*. Some critics called it a masterpiece and others labeled it a pretentious failure. The one thing everyone does agree about is that it is a visually stunning film. Nestor Almendros won an Oscar for his cinematography; but interestingly, it was the only award for which anyone connected with *Days of Heaven* was even nominated. This seems a confirmation of the suggestion that Malick sacrificed too much substance to obtain the visual style that dominates the viewer's experience. Some critics have called it an image film, meaning that it's surface is more important than its content; or to put it another way, that its surface *is* its content. Much of the film is given over to Almendros's beautiful views of the landscape: the luxuriant wheat fields, the endless horizon, the stark outline of a solitary house. (In fact, one reviewer remarked that the actors had to fight against the lush views of wheat fields and that the wheat fields won!)

It is clear that the film that finally emerged from the director's editorial hand was very different from the film the actors thought they had shot. Malick took over a year and a half to edit the film, and some of his choices about what to keep and what to discard were, to say the least, surprising. Richard Gere later commented, "They way we originally shot it, there were major, dramatic passionate scenes, because it's a fucking incredible story, like something by Thomas Hardy. The way scenes are normally constructed, you sort of do elliptical dances until you get into the meat of a scene. What Terry did was, he left in the elliptical dancing and cut out the meat."

There is still a plot of sorts left in *Days of Heaven*—as well as some indication of the movie that might have been shot originally. Richard Gere plays the roll of Bill, whom we first see working in a mill in Chicago. As Gere explained his character, "I play a John Garfield type of punk steelworker from Chicago who runs away from the cops with his girl friend and younger sister and gets lost in the wheat harvest down South. It's about people trying to find some sunshine and some peace in their lives." At first, it seems that they have found what they were looking for in the Texas panhandle, where they work at harvesting a beautiful, golden field of wheat. But they soon learn that the country too has its darker side, as they watch the foreman brutalize the field hands, and see the lumbering farm machinery claim animals as helpless victims.

And, of course, they bring with them their own passions. Bill is obviously a violent man; the reason they left Chicago in the first place was that he punched his supervisor. He sees what he thinks is a perfect opportunity for all three of them when the rich farmer falls in love with his girl friend (for some reason that is never really explained, they have been traveling as brother and sister, disguising their real relationship as lovers). It is common knowledge that the farmer is dying and will have a lot of property to leave behind and a big house with plenty of rooms for everyone, and so Bill urges his girl friend to accept the farmer's proposal of marriage.

But as soon as the trio moves in with the farmer, things begin to go wrong. Not only does the farmer show a deplorable tendency to cling to life, but worse yet, he begins to win the genuine affection of his new wife. Once again, Bill tries to solve his problem through violence, and by the end of the film, both men are dead.

This brief summary gives the impression of more action than the movie itself conveys. Most of the scenes that were meant to advance the plot were left behind on the cutting-room floor, replaced by eye-catching views of the prairie and a chilly voice-over narration by the hero's kid sister, a device that helps to distance the audience even further from their involvement with plot and character. Dialogue is held to a minimum: It's rare that any actor gets to speak more than two or three sentences at a time.

Richard Gere himself has always been warm in his defense of both film and director. "We knew that the movie would be good while we were making it. Some films are more obvious than others. There was never any doubt about

Heaven." He emphasizes that he is "very proud of that film," and he has been articulate in explaining exactly what makes it so special. *"Days of Heaven* got into primal, unconscious territories. Terry was not telling a story about people so much as he was about the universe. Terry is obsessed with innocence. He has a very structured intellect. He's also very child-like. . . . I think it's the childlike thing in Terry that allows a story that can express the intellect."

But it is obvious that Gere's admiration for the film as a whole comes at the expense of his own performance. Whatever the success of the film as a whole, it contains less of Gere's passion and talent than he put into it. He has confessed, "I was having *petit mal* every time Terry would cut. Shivers went through me." His agent, Ed Limato, has stated in no uncertain terms that much of the brilliance of Richard's performance was edited out, never to be seen by film audiences. And Richard added wistfully, "I'd like to buy the stuff that was *not* used and put out my own film, that's what I'd like to do."

The fact that Malick turned the film into a personal statement rather than a vehicle for actors meant that acting performances were never the focus of the reviews of *Days of Heaven.* Certainly the reviews were no particular triumph for Richard Gere. Harold Schonberg did say approvingly, in *The New York Times*, that "Richard Gere, looking as though the genes of the young Gregory Peck and Montgomery Clift had gotten mixed up, gives a sturdy performance as Bill, even if he is too sophisticated to give the impression of a migrant worker." David Denby, in *New York* magazine, was at once more critical and more sympathetic: "Gere's anxious street-hustler's intensity, modeled after DeNiro's manner in *Taxi Driver*, doesn't seem to fit the period at all. (I would bet that some of Gere's anxiety is not conscious acting but frustrated desire to break through the barriers Malick has thrown up around him.)" Several of the most extensive reviews, such as those of Stanley Kauffmann and Pauline Kael, didn't even mention Gere's performance. The one bright spot was the fact that he did win one award for his performance. In the fall of 1979, he was given the Italian film industry's David Donatello award for Best Actor of 1978, based on his performance in *Days of Heaven*. It was surely a satisfaction to him to have his work recognized at last.

It was probably fortunate that once the shooting of *Days of Heaven* was completed, Richard Gere had little time to brood over the final shape the film was taking; nor did he have to worry immediately about critical reaction to his performance, since the final cut would not be released until late in 1978. Instead, he was already busy with his next movie.

For he quickly found a new role. One that would finally bring public attention ... and adulation.

Chapter Five

Public Acclaim

Richard Gere once confessed to a reporter, "I don't vacation well." He worked hard when he was struggling to break into show buisness, and he continued to work just as hard when success finally appeared to be at hand. As soon as Richard finished his work in *Days of Heaven*, he hopped a plane to Los Angeles. He was in hot pursuit of another part, a supporting role in a big film that had every expectation of commercial success.

Once again, casting agent Judy Lamb acted as a fairy godmother to Gere's blossoming career. With a few clips from *Baby Blue Marine* and some rushes from *Days of Heaven*, she approached director Richard Brooks, who was already in the process of shooting his new film.

It was a project that seemed likely to be both exciting and successful. Paramount had acquired the film rights to Judith Rossner's best-selling novel about the perils of the singles-bar scene, the chilling *Looking for Mr. Goodbar*. The studio immediately went after Richard Brooks to direct. He was a veteran screenwriter and director whose credits included *The Blackboard Jungle*, *The Professionals*, and Truman Capote's *In Cold Blood*; he seemed to combine a flair for action pictures with an ability to handle gritty urban settings. Brooks said yes, and quickly began the difficult task of casting the movie. He selected Diane Keaton as the heroine, whose hazardous search for Mr. Right through the singles bars of New York eventually leads to her death. But he had been unable to find the right actor for the key role of Tony Lopanto, the most memorable of the Mr. Wrongs the heroine encounters along the way. Brooks had in fact tried several different young actors in the part, but none of them succeeded in conveying the right combination of sexuality and menace.

Time was running out, and there was no likely candidate in sight ... until Judy Lamb came along touting the talents of Richard Gere. A look at some footage from *Days of Heaven* convinced Brooks that he would like to talk to Gere; Gere in his turn was anxious to work with a director of Brooks's stature, no matter what the project. One interview convinced

Brooks, and his star Diane Keaton, that Gere was the actor they had been searching for. Richard himself remembers the interview as a somewhat difficult event. "I was kind of on edge after three months of Terry [Malick]" he admits. Moreover, he didn't know anything about *Looking for Mr. Goodbar* and had not even read the book. "I thought it was just some cheap piece of crap novel. But I decided to talk to them. Literally, I just walked in and took the part. There wasn't much film on me. Brooks just took me on reputation. He didn't want to futz around spoon-feeding some actor who didn't know when to hit his marks. I told him I wanted to read the script, so what he did was go through the script and just show me my lines. If my line started in the middle of a page, he'd rip off the top of the page so I couldn't read any of the other actors' lines."

Once they got past this slightly paranoid beginning, Gere and Brooks settled down to work extremely well together. Said Gere, "After the first day of shooting, he trusted me totally. He knew I understood the character as well as he did, and I got total support." He later summed up the experience of working on the film: "I had a good time making *Mr. Goodbar*. Diane was wonderful, and I like Richard Brooks. He's crazy and can be incredibly violent . . . but he's also a very talented and sensitive man."

It is hard to imagine any other actor playing

Tony Lopanto, because Richard Gere made the part entirely his own. Tony is the sort of man every woman both hopes and fears to get. He is a street hustler, neither very sophisticated nor articulate. His usual state of inner tension, exacerbated by the drugs he takes, manifests itself in constant movement—drumming fingers, shifting posture, quick flicks of the eyes, and turns of the head. But—and what a but—he is almost unbelievably sexy. Every movement of his body, every glance, even his silences bespeak a powerful sexuality just waiting to be unleashed. What woman could resist?

Certainly not Theresa Dunn, the heroine of the movie. She arrives at the risky decision to take Tony up on his promise to be the best lay of her life, and in an unexpected and unusual fashion, he makes good on his boast. He first virtually terrorizes the woman with an ominous yet erotic dance around the bedroom, wearing only a jock strap and wielding a wicked-looking switchblade before her paralyzed gaze. Just as the sense of menace builds to its height, Tony's mood changes, and he becomes lustfully carnal, rousing Theresa to the highest pitch of ecstasy.

Richard Gere makes the screen image of Tony look easy and natural, but that sense of ease came from a lot of hard work and intense concentration. The sex scenes, Richard's first on the screen, were especially nerve-wracking at first. "I'm not aggressive in real life. I'm very shy. Diane Keaton was shy, too. She was very nervous about the sex scenes. I was nervous about everything. I walked into a film that was already shooting, and I didn't know anybody. Because of my own insecurity, I was very uptight the first day. And she thought I didn't like her or respond to her as an actress, but we worked out our problems and it was a very creative experience. The set was closed, and we improvised a lot."

Richard gives his director full credit for much-needed support and help in those first tense days. "Brooks was the best experience I've ever had. He told me no more than I needed and made me feel supremely confident. There was never any doubt in my mind that here was an incredible human being, working from a very clean place, with no dollar motive at all. He totally changed my ideas about filmmaking." Brooks, in return, has also expressed his admiration for Richard Gere's acting talent. He explains his enormous screen appeal by saying, "There's something unpredictable, even dangerous, about him."

The performance finally made it to the screen with a sizzling and sensual jolt. As journalist Harvey Elliott put it, "Gere created a conduit for Theresa's sexuality that exposed a strong and exciting magnetism in the actor himself. Not all that heat was Tony's." Richard Gere shrewdly put his own finger on one reason for the success of his appearance as Tony: "Knowing Tony wasn't the real killer made it easy to be as ugly or outrageous as I wanted to be, because I knew the audience would end up loving me."

God knows he was right—they did. The film was released in October, 1977, and public response was immediate. Tony Lopanto was the man they loved to hate, and Richard Gere was the actor they wanted to see more of (in every sense of the word). Most of the reviews concentrated on the performance of Diane Keaton, here playing a role that was a big departure from what viewers usually associated her with. Richard Gere commented perceptively, "I think the critics would have liked the film better if it had starred anyone other than Diane Keaton. People have so many preconceived ideas about her that they felt she was violated by the film, and therefore they were violated by the film, too."

But even though he was only on the screen for about fifteen minutes, Richard Gere also received a lot of critical attention. He was called "convincing" and "electric," and Vincent Canby said he was "especially good." Frank Rich didn't like the film, but he did like Gere, saying,"Only the Italian stud, Tony, played with magnificent ferocity by Richard Gere, seems remotely human." Stephen Farber, in *New West* magazine, praised, "Gere is like a more handsome Robert

DeNiro; he burns up the screen and embodies the idea of sex as pure energy." The most perceptive analysis of Gere's performance appeared several years later, in an article in *Film Comment* by Stephen Harvey: "There's no denying the impact of his first conspicuous movie performance—as Diane Keaton's dense, carnal, almost comically sensitive stud in *Looking for Mr. Goodbar*. Much of it, of course, had to do with his brute-boyish, hyperkinetic physical appeal (particularly in the sequence commemorated by aficionados as The Jock Strap Scene). Even more persuasive, though, was the fact that, however souped-up and perfervid the context may have been, Gere was working in harmony with the movie's intentions. His character's libidinous menace was transmitted through Keaton's alternately fearful and amused reaction to it before reaching us out there in the audience. And it worked, because these two performers created this tension in concert."

Earlier that year, when Terence Malick finally decided to cast Richard Gere in a starring role in *Days of Heaven*, he warned him, "It's going to change your life." He was right in principle, although wrong about the specifics. Since *Days of Heaven* wasn't released until late in 1978, it was in fact *Looking for Mr. Goodbar* that changed Richard Gere's life. It gave him immediate public recognition, and it also gave him an image that he later found hard to shake. Many of his fans—indeed, even many people in the movie business—found it hard to separate Richard Gere from Tony Lopanto. He told Rex Reed, "People bug me; nuts call me up in the middle of the night. They're cooler about it in New York, but they still expect me to be a punk." Perhaps that's why he chose to stay on in his old apartment, surrounded by the familiar faces of old friends and longtime residents (predominantly Puerto Rican). "They didn't see *Goodbar*. Those people don't go to movies. Somebody tells them. I could be anything—a politician or a pimp. Your name and your picture get into the paper and they start giggling."

It wasn't giggling Richard heard from the rest of the world, but the sound of heavy breathing. He was pursued, telephoned, all but literally drooled over when he went out in public. Fans hung around hoping to get a glimpse of him, and they even began to bother his family in Syracuse. Richard Gere found that suddenly becoming a sex symbol was an alarming experience. "I talked to nobody. I refused to do publicity interviews. Things moved so fast I felt like the Flavor of the Month. I just couldn't take it." But he was amused to find that not everyone recognized him immediately, even if they had seen him on the screen. "Right after the release of *Goodbar*, I took a vacation at a Holiday Inn. One morning I was in the coffee shop, and two guys next to me were talking. They were going on about my performance. I was wearing the same jacket, I had the same look I'd had in the movie, and they weren't picking up on it. Finally I told them who I was and they didn't believe me." The experience led him to a very useful conclusion. "I think if you don't go around in a limousine with bodyguards, you can get away with a lot."

The other, perhaps more important, way that *Looking for Mr. Goodbar* brought change to the life of Richard Gere was its effect on his career. Suddenly, he had offers coming in from all directions. Most of them, of course, were for roles that were very similar to Tony Lopanto. Gere comments, "After *Goodbar*, I had enough offers to play Italian crazies for the next fifteen years. The bastards want to put you in a box with a label on it and crush it. If you have any hope of growing, of being taken seriously, you have to control the vultures." Richard was determined to avoid being typecast, and he also wanted to make sure each of his future roles offered him some new challenge as an actor. So he turned down all the Italian crazies. Interestingly, he also turned down the lead in *Midnight Express*; he thought the violence in the film was gratuitous and that it lacked any sort of real significance.

RICHARD GERE

It took a lot of determination, and he made some enemies in the process, but Richard Gere succeeded in preventing the cheap exploitation of his newfound fame.

Chapter Six

While the Iron Is Hot

"You wanna know how success has changed me?" explained Richard Gere in January of 1978. "When you start out acting, you just want to work. You're not concerned with the messages of the pieces or the motives of the people making them. As I've been given more responsibility in a medium that is seen by millions and has a tremendous influence on the psyche of the world, I find myself choosing projects that are something I can believe in morally."

Of the many scripts that were submitted to Gere after his sizzling portrayal of Tony, few lived up to his standards. Not only was he looking for meaningful roles, but also he wanted roles that would encourage his growth, both as an actor and as a human being. "I'm trying to be different each time," he confided. "If people have an image of you, it's like voodoo. They stick a pin in you, like a butterfly, and you die."

In the course of the year following the release of *Looking for Mr. Goodbar*, Gere did find two films that met his highest standards. The first project he became interested in was a movie called *Bloodbrothers*. It was based on a modestly successful novel by Richard Price, and was being made by Warner Brothers. The director of the film was Robert Mulligan, who had previously received critical acclaim for his work in *Love with the Proper Stranger* and *To Kill a Mockingbird*. Walter Newman, whose credits included the screenplay for *Cat Ballou*, was hired to produce an adaptation of the novel for the screen. Mulligan had assembled an excellent supporting cast, including Broadway veterans Tony Lo Bianco, Paul Sorvino, and Lelia Goldoni. All he needed was a star.

The leading role in *Bloodbrothers* is the part of Stony De Coco, an eighteen-year-old boy on the brink of manhood who is torn between his desire to live up to his father's expectations of him and become a member of the macho world of construction workers, and his own desire to express the gentler side of his nature by working with children: a desire that is probably rooted in his fierce protectiveness of his younger brother who is a victim of their parents' repressed hostilities. Presumably Richard Gere came to mind as a candidate for the role because he had already shown his ability to combine both tough and tender elements in a performance . . . and possibly also because Stony De Coco was, like Tony Lopanto, an Italian-American boy from a working-class background.

The problem, it seemed, was that at twenty-eight, Richard Gere was simply too old for the role. He was a decade older than the part he would play, and Mulligan definitely wanted a younger actor. Gere, too, had his reservations about playing so young and unformed a character; he described Stony as "an eighteen-year-old innocent who hadn't made any major decisions, when in reality I had—anyway, more than that kid had." But somehow, no other actor seemed to Mulligan to bring to the part what Richard Gere could, and so finally Gere was signed to star in *Bloodbrothers*.

Mulligan decided, for the sake of realism, to shoot the film on location in New York, in the parts of the Bronx in which the action is set. So Richard Gere was able to hang out in the city and observe some real-life Stonys. He explained how he was able to play so convincingly the part of a boy with a background so different from his own: "I've lived in Manhattan seven years, and you know, you try people out. You study types. I'm always studying men on the street, in bars, everywhere. That's what my job is. On a specific character, I search out what I need for the job. Actors are always sucking up everything that's going on." In fact, Gere did such a good job of assuming the personality of Stony that he later confessed, "It took me a long time to get rid of that guy."

Although Richard Gere is without question the star of *Bloodbrothers*, the movie has a strong ensemble, thanks to the talented actors Gere had the chance to play against. This is especially true in his scenes with the two acting veterans who play his father (Tony Lo Bianco) and his uncle (Paul Sorvino). Richard remembers that the film's schedule gave time for the cast to get to know one another before the shooting actually started, and that led to a sense of ease among the players that is visible on the screen. Everything about the movie was carefully planned and then just as carefully rehearsed, so there was little room left for the sort of improvisation Gere had been called upon to produce in his earlier films. "All the elements worked in *Bloodbrothers*," commented its star. "Everything flowed. It was clear what was happening all the time."

Robert Mulligan has been called an actor's director, meaning that he concentrates first and foremost on allowing his actors all the conditions they need to perform. Gere says, "The style of the shooting is indicated by what part of the soul it's coming from. Bob was photographing performances in *Bloodbrothers*, basically. Very simple emotional situations within a family. Therefore, it was mostly in close-up— seeing people's eyes." He adds, "I like Bob Mulligan a lot. As an actor, I think I enjoyed working with him and Richard Brooks the best. They're both very supportive and instill great confidence in the actor."

What was Richard Gere's assessment of the movie when it was finished? *"Bloodbrothers* has a lot of heart. It's a simple, straight-ahead emotional opera. I liked that. I went with it." He continued on a more personal note, "My brother David saw it when he visited me in England and we had a screening. He wept. That made me happy. So I certainly feel it was a worthwhile film."

Certainly, some aspects of Richard Gere's performance in the movie are very affecting. Richard Price, author of the novel on which the film was based, recollected one such moment. "There's a scene in *Bloodbrothers* in which Gere, playing a hospital attendant, tells a room full of eight-year-old kids a ghost story. He speaks in a playful, spook-house whisper, and the kids are pop-eyed with fascination. By the end of his tale, he's turned it into an allegory of brotherhood. Despite the potential bathos of that scene, he received a spontaneous standing ovation when the film was shown at the New York Film Festival. Sweetness and earnestness might not make an audience horny, but it can warm people—it can get them on your side. Sex doesn't last, but cooking does." Gere was the recipient of a similar standing ovation when the film premiered in California.

But many professional critics were less impressed. One of the kindest reviews was from Harold Schonberg in *The New York Times*. "There is a notable bit of miscasting, too, in Richard Gere as Stony De Coco, the sensitive son. By no freak of genetics could he have come from the lines of his parents. Gere is a fine young actor with immense charm, but he is not believable in this role. He has to cope with too many artificial and predictable situations, and not even he can overcome the stylistic, contrived qualities of the role and the picture." *Time*'s critic was somewhat harsher. "As for Richard Gere, the jury is still out. . . . He is a powerful sexual presence. His scenes with the film's child actors are convincingly tender. But bad habits plague him: He affects too many Brando pauses, De Niro stutterings, and Travolta grins. He may yet become a Somebody in the movies, but not until he stops acting like everybody else."

Some of the other critics seemed to be reviewing Richard Gere rather than his performance in *Bloodbrothers*. *New York* magazine's David Denby said, "As Stony, Richard Gere gives an excitingly kinetic performance, but there's more energy than personality in Gere's work. I know that Stony is supposed to be searching for himself, but that's no reason for Gere to be searching for his identity as an actor. There's a vacancy in his eyes that hurts his performances; you reach out to make contact with his characters . . . and you see only good looks, ambition, and an actor trying awfully hard for sex appeal (actually he's more jumpy than sexy)." Stephen Harvey was nastier: "*Bloodbrothers* was grandstanding. . . . This *Saturday Night Fever Goes Grand Guignol* should have been surefire overnight-star material; Gere's role is achingly sympathetic, with a set piece featuring Gere surrounded by adoring, vulnerable kiddies, compared to which Irene Dunne in *Love Affair* would resemble *Annie's* Miss Hannigan. Yet Gere stifled the character by working too hard at winning over the audience's affections." Worst of all was Pauline Kael's epigrammatic comment: "Richard Gere is to Robert De Niro as *Beatlemania* is to the Beatles."

Bloodbrothers was not any more successful at the box office than it was with the critics. It grossed less than $1 million, which made it a financial flop, earning less than it cost to make.

Bloodbrothers was a relatively quick shoot, but even so, Richard Gere had very little free time before he was scheduled to start work on his next project. It was being shot on location in England, so he went to London and settled down near Hyde Park in a cozy flat that he sublet from the actress Jan Sterling. As it turned out, the shooting lasted more than eight months, so he didn't return to the U.S. until nearly the end of 1978.

The new film was called *Yanks*, and it was a story about wartime that left out the war. Gere summed it up: "It's about people in transit, not knowing what's happening the next day, and about the fear of committing themselves under those circumstances." The film was set in 1943, in the darkest days of World War II, when American troops were beginning to arrive in England as part of the big buildup that would eventually lead to the invasion of Normandy. The plot follows the romances of three different American soldiers and the women they meet in England. At one end of the spectrum is an aristocratic Englishwoman, played by Vanessa Redgrave, who has an affair with an American officer (William Devane). At the other end is a cheerfully immoral bus conductor (Wendy Morgan) and her boyfriend, a former prizefighter who is now a cook in the Army (Chick Venners). The couple in between these two extremes, and the one on whom most of the movie is focused, is played by Richard Gere as a decent, small-town boy who is serving his country as a mess sergeant, and Lisa Eichhorn, the innocent daughter of the local postmaster.

Yanks was directed by John Schlesinger, whose previous successes included *Midnight*

Cowboy; Sunday, Bloody Sunday; and *Marathon Man*. He was the one who initiated the project and then tried to find backing for it. He commented, "It was hell, getting financing for *Yanks*." In the end, he managed to raise $7.5 million, quite a respectable sum. He hired two screenwriters: Colin Welland from England and Walter Bernstein from America, to make sure the viewpoints of both countries were accurately represented. Schlesinger cast his film with great care. Of course, signing a big-name star with guaranteed bankability would have helped him get the money in the first place, but he was convinced that Richard Gere was the actor who would do the best job with the part. He said he set out to find a "reincarantion of Gary Cooper in the forties," and someone suggested that he consider Gere. Schlesinger remembered seeing *Looking for Mr. Goodbar*, and recalled that he hadn't cared for the film but found Gere's performance arresting. So he arranged to meet with Richard several times, giving them the chance to talk seriously and sum each other up. Schlesinger said, "I talked to everyone: Pacino, Hoffman. Gere was the freshest, most interesting actor for the part. There was a complexity there that hasn't been tapped in his previous films. A sensitivity and beauty in a way. A quality that Montgomery Clift had."

For a man of Richard Gere's age (twenty-eight at the time) *Yanks* was truly a period piece; after all, he hadn't even been born in 1943. So he worked hard at preparing for his role. First he went out to Arizona, which was supposed to be his character's home state; he wanted to know what sort of a life his hero had led before he was drafted. His next step is an even better indicator of the meticulousness of his attention to the details of his character's existence. "I went to Fort Dix, New Jersey, and did what I was doing in the movie. I worked with the mess sergeant, who was very flattered and proud as he showed me around the kitchen." The final stage of his preparation for the role was to talk to his father. "He had been in the service when he was about the same age as the boy in *Yanks*. He came from a small town, too—a farmboy tied to the earth. The simplicity of life was strong in my father and still is. And that's a quality lost to us today." He added thoughtfully, "I had never played somebody as boyish and normal."

Richard Gere elaborated on that image of his character in another interview, before the film was released. "All the characters I play are pretty extreme, but the one in *Yanks* was more a stripping-away. The critics are going to hate me. I knew what I was doing. There was a kind of . . . innocence to the character. I think of the way my father must have been. It's a whole point of view that's alien to us, an uncynical view. These guys were pulled out of small towns without knowing anything, and suddenly found themselves playing for high stakes. There is a certain openness in their eyes." And he revealed to an interviewer from *The New York Times* that he had also prepared for the part by studying old photographs of his father in his Navy uniform. "I often use photographs to prepare for a part," he explained. "They can tell you everything about a character, the way he stands, the environment he works in. All these elements build up to the central core of what a man is all about." There is something endearing about the frankness of Richard Gere's identification of his father with his character (Matt). "Matt really reminded me a lot of my father. My father has the same openness and honesty, and a basic willingness to take responsibility, just as Matt takes emotional responsibility for the girl." Interestingly, his parents were quick to notice the resemblance; when the Geres went to visit their son on the set in England, his mother burst into tears when she saw how much like his father he looked in his costume uniform.

But as much as Richard Gere liked playing the part of Matt, he found making the movie a draining experience. The hours were long, for one thing, especially since he had to commute back and forth to the location outside Bradford, where an enormous army base had been reconstructed. According to one interview at the time, "Gere virtually slinks home from the set each weekday evening, falls into a deep coma, is awakened by the alarm the following morning, only to be driven by limousine to a location site where the process is repeated ad infinitum."

Yanks was also an emotionally tiring film. Gere explained: "It was a very difficult film because I had to cut away every contemporary distraction and transfer my mind to 1943 for seven months. I had to remove myself from me and project my thoughts into a more innocent time that no longer exists. I did a lot of research, brooding, and thinking." He added, "Sometimes films are hell to make. *Yanks* is more difficult because it's so large and sometimes you feel you're not getting a focus. The actors are not in control of what's going down."

Richard Gere did not intend these remarks to be a criticism of the director, John Schlesinger. To the contrary, he came away from the project with respect for Schlesinger's professionalism. "You look at his films and you say, well, every one of his performers is great. And you'd think that he talks a lot, but he really doesn't. He's very concerned with all that, but he's also very concerned with camera and image. Again, it comes off fine. Look at the film. You just have to trust someone like John, that in the end it will all work—and it does. John's very good that way. He has a very classical sense of the marriage of the two—performance and image.

His narrative style is wonderful, he's a great storyteller." He concludes firmly, "I think the film turned out well. Schlesinger devotes so much time, care, and sensitivity to details. No other director could have done it. He's very precise about what he wants. You can look at his work and know this is a man who knows about film."

By the time *Yanks* was released, in the fall of 1979, expectations for the movie were very high. It had taken so long to film; so much care and patience had gone into even the tiniest details of the production; there were good performances by a number of fine actors. Pundits predicted a smash for Universal Studios—and a breakout film for Richard Gere.

They were wrong.

The film grossed only $3 million at the box office, less than half of what it cost to make. And although many critics did praise Gere's performance, most of them were only lukewarm about the film, and some even concluded that the odd sense of hollowness at the core of it was due in part to the restraint of Gere's portrayal of Matt. He was called "sympathetic" and "appealing"; "endearing and accomplished"; and even those who criticized the performance sometimes recognized the talent that underlied it. For example, Jack Kroll, in *Newsweek*, said, "Gere is a good young actor who hasn't quite exploded into a vivid personality." Gary Arnold (*The Washington Post*) added, "Gere profits from the inherent likability of Matt without really enlarging on the potential of the character. Something is missing, and you feel that its absence prevents both the movie and the characterization from going decisively over the top." Vincent Canby, in *The New York Times*, criticized gently, "Mr. Gere underplays his role as if the movie were going to take up the slack and give his physical presence some sort of emotional impact. It doesn't." Stephen Harvey concluded, "*Yanks* cast Gere in another saintly underdog part, in which he did his most subtly inflected, least self-indulgent movie acting to date. Unfortunately, his work as the lovelorn GI was *so* controlled as to seem positively inert. The memories one retains of the performance are fleeting, struck attitudes—hunched shoulders and wincing eyes tensed against the sodden Yorkshire breeze and the prospect of romantic disillusionment."

It must all have been a bit discouraging for Richard Gere. He had made four major films in quick succession, working with four well-known and talented directors, each of whom had already turned out at least one extremely successful movie. For a relative unknown, just getting such parts might be counted a triumph. He commented, "I started getting hired to do films before anyone knew who I was. I suppose they just thought I was a good actor. And I was working with directors who could get projects going without major movie stars. We all just wanted to get the best job done that we possibly could." But somehow, even with those four good opportunities, lightning failed to strike. He got some good reviews, and the moviegoing public was beginning to recognize his name and face. But he still wasn't a star. And he still wasn't a bankable actor. He recognized the truth. "If there's a $15 million film, and there's no zappy stuff—no disco or whatever it is at the moment—they've got to have someone who pulls them in. Sure, there are some projects that I wanted to do but couldn't because of that situation."

In many ways, it was a frustrating time in his life.

Chapter Seven

The Pressures of Stardom

"I'm trying to keep my own soul together. I don't want to get an image that won't allow me to change and grow. I don't want my privacy projected upon by the public." That's Richard Gere speaking, early in 1978. The quote gives an indication of some of the pressures he was already starting to feel, at a time when only *Looking for Mr. Goodbar* had been released. A year later, with *Days of Heaven* and *Bloodbrothers* just out, and *Yanks* soon to come, the pressures, of course, had greatly increased. It all happened so fast that Gere had still not developed very successful strategies for coping with it. The strain often showed.

It is hard for those of us who haven't experienced it to comprehend the magnitude of change that Hollywood fame can bring to an actor's life. On January 1, 1977, Richard Gere was still Mr. Nobody. His name was recognized only by the small group of hard-core fans who keep off-Broadway and regional theater alive. Just one year later, "Offers are pouring in, people are talking about percentages, grosses, development deals, director approval. It's too much for me to deal with."

Many talented young performers have been destroyed by these pressures. Hollywood is infamous for its "Me Too" mentality. When you are an unknown, your phone never rings; in fact, you can't even get people to take your calls. But once word starts to spread that you're hot, everyone wants you. Even if they've never seen you before. Even if the part's all wrong for you. Even if they don't actually *have* a part written yet. They all want you, but they don't even know who *you* are. It's easy to understand why the experience leaves so many performers feeling exploited and angry, or why they so quickly become cynical and hostile in return.

In certain ways, Richard Gere was especially vulnerable to the problems of sudden success, because his system of values was in direct conflict with that of Hollywood and its mass-market appeal. As he confessed to Rex Reed, he still saw himself as "an actor with an off-Broadway mentality." That meant that he cared about his craft; that he wanted to make good films, personal films, films that stood for something. It meant that he wasn't easily seduced by the usual bribes of cars, houses, a trendy lifestyle. To the contrary, he was actively suspicious of such involvement with the purely material. "Having money presents possibilities, but it also presents dangers. If you buy a lifestyle and then have to maintain it, they've got you again." Most of all it meant that when Richard Gere was willing to be open about his ambitions and aspirations, he was very frequently misunderstood. For example, *People* ran a quote, in late 1977, from Gere, in which he said, "I want power, power to express myself—I want to be somebody, but I don't want to have to screw anybody over to get there," but had the snide headlines "The power of naive thinking." Gere summed up the problem flatly: "Most of my ideas are too esoteric for Hollywood."

It was probably inevitable that Richard Gere would be hurt in the process of becoming a star. And although he might deny the extent of his vulnerability, it is clear that he knew he was affected by it, that he understood he couldn't escape untouched. Years later, he told his *Breathless* co-star, Valerie Kaprisky, a little about the way he had felt. "He told me that he was very friendly and open in the beginning of his career and was very disappointed with what happened. He's afraid of people, and when you're afraid of people, you're agressive."

The best impression of Gere in those early years of his stardom has been set down by novelist Richard Price, who wrote about meeting him in his Village street-front apartment when he was working on *Bloodbrothers*. "When he finally emerged, Gere was wearing his finest BVDs and smoking a cigarette that hung from his lips in a Belmondo vertical drop. He mumbled 'hey,' gave me a hug, and dropped on the couch as if he were suffering from combat fatigue. . . . From the minute he made his entrance, the room seemed to shrink to the dimensions of a broom closet. It had nothing to do with his glamour or physicality. It was something deeper, more anxiety-provoking. He projected a furtive alertness, an acute self-consciousness, with a mind that never stopped checking out the scene. . . . I felt that it was important to Gere that I liked him and was taken with him. I felt he was wooing me, offering himself. But despite the obviousness of his deciding to enter a room in his BVDs to meet a stranger, it wasn't sexual. And it was a successful woo; not because of the preening and the schtick, but because the preening and the schtick were so humanly transparent. He seemed so self-consumed, so self-conscious, that he laid out more cards on the table than he realized. In his own ass-backward way, he was one of the most honest and open people I'd ever met. I liked him tremendously."

Interviewer and film critic Joseph Gelmis, of *Newsday*, wrote about another of Richard Gere's open moments, when he tried honestly to explain how he felt about his sudden fame. "Somewhere along the line you grab the brass ring and you want to let go, but you can't, because you're going too fast. You feel like you're going to fall right on your head if you let go. So you hold on. And it keeps passing faster and faster. And you're holding on. And then someone grabs hold of your legs. And you get more and more people holding on. . . . Soon you've got fifteen people, and then you've got thousands of people, and you're holding on even more. And you can't let go, 'cause you'll die if you let go. It's just total lunacy. You're caught in between."

Gere is expressing very graphically one of the most frightening aspects of sudden stardom: the sense of no longer being in control of one's own life. He commented sadly, "You people in media have control. You can solidify concepts and personas so they can be marketed. . . . It's false." Like many people in such a situation, he tried to combat his anxiety by exerting even more control over other areas of existence. He tried to shun all interviews and publicity. Although he hired a personal publicist, her chief assignment was to protect him from the press (as well as from importunate fans). The only publicity photographs he would allow to be released were taken by a close friend, rather than a stranger whose intentions he might not be able to gauge. He demanded that journalists be kept off the set when he was working. When the press did penetrate his wall of privacy, he let them see his anger and hostility. He left parties abruptly when he discovered lurking photogs, and he often exchanged angry insults with paparazzi.

Journalists, of course, were quick to resent such an attitude. They started to harp in print on his sullenness, his arrogance, his seeming condescension. The very same reporters who had been raving about him began to demand, "Who does he think he is?" Said *Village Voice* columnist Arthur Bell, an early Gere booster, "He's trying to come on like Greta Garbo and Sylvia Miles at the same time." Rex Reed accused him of "carrying the Greta Garbo mystique to ridiculous proportions. If he's not careful, nobody will want to talk to him at all." Everyone agreed it was all right for a superstar like Brando to act like that, but for an upstart like Richard Gere to give himself such airs . . .

It took Richard Gere several years to work through this dilemma in both his public and his private life. On the one hand, he genuinely did not want to give personal interviews, resented the prying into his privacy, was annoyed that so much attention was focused on the person instead of the work. On the other hand, he was shrewd enough to realize that his popularity with those very fans who wanted to know so many personal details about his life was the source of his power. Only mass appeal at the box office could give him the ability to pick and choose among decent scripts, perhaps even to find financial backing for projects of his own initiation. Moreover, he recognized that his own silence was in large part the reason he had been typecast as a sullen punk. He hadn't given the public the opportunity to see any of the other sides of Richard Gere; all they knew was what they saw on the screen, in a succession of parts in which he portrayed alienated, violent men.

So he gave journalists the interviews, but at the same time, he let them see his contempt for the whole process. One of them wrote, "He would clearly rather be somewhere else, perhaps at his dentist's undergoing a little root canal work." Another commented, "He seems to reserve for interviews the sentiments a dog has for flea baths." His love-hate relationship with the press achieved its moment of ultimate expression when he was being interviewed by a writer for *The Ladies' Home Journal*. She asked the tactless question, "How does it feel to be a sex object?" he responded by saying, "This is what I call a sex object," and dropping his pants. Today, Richard Gere laughs as he recalls that the writer "looked down matter-of-factly and said, 'Oh, I've seen better.' " Needless to say, the story never ran in the magazine!

In his private life, too, Richard Gere seemed to experience that same kind of alternating push and pull. He chose to go out to public places, where he would surely be recognized and photographed—and then became explosively angry when it happened. Richard Price described this mechanism at work when he bumped into Richard Gere at a party in 1979. Price recalled, "It seemed that at least half the people standing around us were staring at him out of the corners of their eyes with what seemed to be a mixture of anger and awe. . . . Gere has always had the power to demand that you watch him. . . . He was incapable of looking unaware of the people around him, incapable of projecting stay-away vibes. And now, in this room, it was as if he were holding everyone's neck in a noose at the end of a pole. They couldn't get too close and they couldn't walk away. But neither could he. Gere tried to come off as though he were oblivious to all this tension, but the unsmiling tightness of his mouth betrayed him. . . . I couldn't imagine he had come to the party in anticipation of a good time. The night seemed like some blind foray into the combat zone. If Gere had exploded at that party, I don't know if he would have screamed, 'I hate you' or 'Why don't you love me?' "

All these psychological pressures were no doubt exacerbated by the speed with which the circumstances of Richard Gere's daily life changed because of his success. One significant change was the breakup of his relationship with Penelope Milford. She had been an integral part of his "off-Broadway actor's" mentality; she shared and encouraged the value system that put art and self-expression ahead of commerce and material gain. When Gere was still involved with Milford, he told a reporter sincerely, "I know I could walk away from this, and I would be so happy. I could go to a Zen monastery. If I could spend the rest of my life making little things with my lady up in the woods, I'd be okay." But the long separation while Richard was in England shooting *Yanks*, and perhaps also the pressures of his commercial success, put a strain on the relationship that caused it to founder. No five-year relationship ends easily; and although neither of them has ever discussed the split publicly, it seems safe to conclude that in separating from Milford, Gere relinquished a source of emotional security and even self-definition that had been very important to him.

Success also brought a big change in the material circumstances of his life. He was able to give up the cheap apartment in a questionable neighborhood—a sensible decision, of course, but one more rip in the fabric of the familiar daily life. He described his state of mind: "I'm as open as I can be to what my next impulse is. Before I started *Yanks*, I got rid of my apartment and the beach house I was renting near Hollywood. I own a couple of guitars, one on each coast, and some clothes. Something's going to happen within the month, I suppose, but meanwhile it's chaos." Although it seems unlikely that Richard Gere is ever going to turn into an all-American consumer, possessions are not the only things that money can buy. Travel, privacy, insulation from the daily cares of life; in short, freedom, which can, in its own way, be as addictive as houses or cars. And it can take some getting used to.

But it would be silly to overstress the difficulties of success. Richard Gere was by no means a pathetic prisoner of his fame, but an ambitious young man struggling to build a career and at the same time exert some control over it. There is no doubt about his commitment to his career and to some very specific career goals. He knew that only success would bring him the power to make the kinds of films he was really interested in. He summed it up: "The only answer is to keep making viable commercial films with good directors and hope my so-called Hollywood name will make me a good enough risk to make films like Herrzog on my own."

In truth, Gere's commitment to career success ran even deeper than his desire to exert control over the roles he played. There was a part of him that wanted to be noticed, wanted to be admired, wanted the pure thrill of being a Star. He said it himself, in a remarkably honest comment: "That movie star thing is the highest role I know about. It's frightening. Yet I don't want to avoid it, though a part of me finds it repulsive. Perfection that will not allow interaction is not perfection. You've got to be able to take it all and transform it for it to be paradise."

Chapter Eight
Playing the Gigolo

"The more you learn about this business, you realize the most important thing is control. The control to do what you want to do. That's what I'm working toward. . . ." But that degree of control still eluded Richard Gere. Look at what happened, early in 1979, when he found a part that he really wanted to play.

Gere heard about the project from the man who wrote it, Paul Schrader. Schrader, acclaimed for the powerful screenplay of *Taxi Driver*, spent all of 1976 in a veritable creative frenzy, producing five finished scripts. Faced with such an embarrassment of riches, he realized he couldn't possibly find the time himself to follow up on all five projects, so he decided to sell several to major studios for development, while directing others himself. One of the scripts he sold was called *American Gigolo*.

Schrader claims that the genesis of the script was a conversation with students in the screen-writing class he taught at UCLA. They were talking about occupations that might create cinematic interest, and a student mentioned the word gigolo. Schrader, for some reason, added a national identity: "American gigolo." The very next day, the phrase came to his mind again, as he was discussing with his psychia-trist the fact that it can sometimes be harder to receive love than it is to give it. He says, "When you give something, you can distance yourself from it, just stand above it. When you receive something, it calls for more parti-cipation with the person who's giving, to show appreciation. . . . The notion of the gigolo as a metaphor for the man who can't receive pleasure hit me, and from that moment on I had a meta-phor that was uniquely representative of that problem. Then it was just a matter of plotting it out."

Schrader found a willing buyer for the script of *American Gigolo* in producer Freddie Fields at Paramount. For the next several years, while Schrader directed two of his other scripts (*Blue Collar* and *Hard Core*), Fields tried to get the project moving at Paramount. But it was not until late in 1978 that it looked like the idea would turn into a reality, and by that time, Schrader was free to direct it himself.

Paul Schrader insists that his first choice for the leading role of Julian Kay was always Richard Gere. He thought Gere had the looks and the magnetic intensity of his gigolo/hero. He sent Gere a script and they began talking enthusiastically about the project. Initially, the Paramount powers were willing to go along with Schrader's choice. But then they thought about the recent huge success of *Saturday Night Fever*, and then they told each other that Richard Gere and John Travolta were really the same type; after all, in the past they had sometimes been up for the same role, and now they had a sexy subject that could be big box office. And so they decided: They wanted Travolta. Apparently they made him an offer he couldn't refuse, and so the part was unceremoniously yanked away from Richard Gere. Gere later said honestly that he felt like "murder, sheer murder," but, of course, it's the sort of disappointment all actors must learn to accept. Gere tried to put it out of his mind and began to look around for something else. He was talking of playing Shakespeare's *Coriolanus*; and he'd heard about an interesting script being developed from a magazine article called *Urban Cowboy*. Something would turn up. . . .

Meanwhile, back at Paramount, *American Gigolo* had been allocated a $9 million budget, thanks to the studio's faith in Travolta's drawing power at the box office. For a movie that was to be shot entirely in southern California, that was a very lavish budget. Schrader flew to Rome and hired famed set designer Ferdinando Scarfiotti to create a series of opulent backgrounds: the hero's Westwood apartment; the Polo Lounge; a beach house in Malibu for the society woman (played by Nina van Pallandt), who makes the gigolo's "arrangements" with her friends and acquaintances. In fact, the sets alone cost more than $1 million. John Bailey, a cinematographer who had worked under Nestor Almendros on *Days of Heaven*, was signed to shoot the film, and he was promptly encouraged to spend time and money experimenting with unusual lighting effects. Chic designer Giorgio Armani produced an elaborate wardrobe suitable for a high-class West Coast lounge lizard, and another haute couture designer, Basile, turned out the clothes for the heroine. She was to be played by fashion model-turned-actress Lauren Hutton.

All the elements of a glossy, slick-looking film were in place. But before the shooting could begin, John Travolta got cold feet about the role and the film. According to Schrader, "John liked the title, liked the clothes, liked the poster, but he was afraid he would fall on his face. When *Moment by Moment* failed, he was just too damned scared it would happen again." Schrader immediately turned to Richard Gere, but he could give the actor only two days to decide, since the film was all set to go into production. Gere said yes. "I never consciously thought about becoming a sex symbol when I accepted the part. But I suppose if you want to be up there—as a movie star, rock star, whatever—part of that is, yes, you want to be desired. And I suppose that is basically sexual. I wouldn't say I did the movie specifically for that reason, but it's part of wanting to be up there, of wanting to be watched and appreciated."

Once he had made his decision, Gere had only ten days to prepare for the part—and a lot of work to do, since in many ways Julian Kay was the direct antithesis of Richard Gere. His first concern was for the specific details of behavior and appearance that would go into the characterization. For example, he had to learn to be comfortable in the stylish wardrobe of the gigolo. "I had never really been concerned with dressing before: jeans, a T-shirt, and a leather jacket were enough. So it wasn't particularly easy for me to get into the style aspect of *Gigolo*. Emotionally, I knew what it was all about, but not stylistically. I had to go to stores. I had to read *Gentlemen's Quarterly*. I did a lot of research. Photographs are incredibly evocative for me. The right photograph can reveal a character very strongly to me." Applying his usual concentration, he learned quickly how to tie a tie, get in and out of a car, wear his clothes with a casual air. "I fairly quickly came to the point where I could make the same decisions Julian would about clothes, about books. I knew what would be around Julian's bed lying out open, how his table would be set." Understanding Julian's psyche was even easier for Gere. He recognized intuitively that Julian's occupation was primarily a metaphor for his emotional condition.

Director Schrader was delighted to be working with an actor who put so much effort in understanding—virtually *becoming*—his character. "When Richard got involved, I got back to making a real movie again, a story about people, themes. In one day, Richard asked all the questions John hadn't asked in six months." In many ways, Schrader now had the best of both worlds: a production budgeted for a star of Travolta's box office appeal and a leading man of Gere's talent and dedication. For the studio, too, there were certain compensations in the replacement of Travolta by Gere. He was paid only $350,000 plus a small percentage of the profits, whereas Travolta had been promised over $1 million. They no longer had to allocate the money to support a large entourage for the star; another saving came from the fact that they could demand a schedule of only fifty days of shooting rather than the sixty they had planned for

Richard Gere—up close and personal—and gorgeous.
(Globe Photos)

One of Richard's ways to relax is playing the piano.
(Globe Photos)

The Bloodbrothers: Paul Sorvino, Gere, Tony Lo Bianco.

A bare-chested Richard Gere in a romantic interlude with Lisa Eichhorn from *Yanks*. (M. Childers/Sygma)

Gere played an American soldier, here doing a little k.p. duty, in *Yanks*.

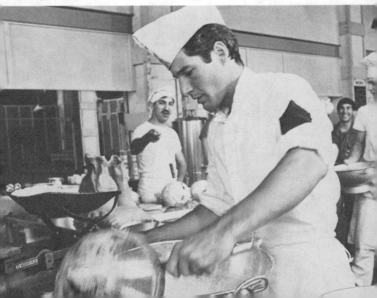

Gere's brooding good looks and perfect body—on view extensively in *American Gigolo*—made him one of today's hottest stars. (M. Childers/Sygma)

Left: In his Georgio Armani duds, Richard Gere set female pulses racing as Julian Kay in *American Gigolo*. (M. Childers/Sygma)

Whether he was being punished by Drill Instructor
Louis Gossett, Jr. (*above*), or pleased by sultry Debra Winger
(*below*), Gere was outstanding in *An Officer and a Gentleman*.

Left: On screen as Julian Kay, or off-screen as himself, Gere
takes good care of his body—with obviously terrific results.
(M. Childers/Sygma)

Wild, zany, incredibly sexy, deliciously romantic, that was Gere in his role as Jesse Lujack in *Breathless*.

Travolta. There were some hard economic realities underlying the difference in the studio's treatment of Gere and Travolta. Most important was the fact that the *combined* gross of Richard Gere's three starring films (*Days of Heaven*, *Bloodbrothers*, and *Yanks*) was less than the gross of Travolta's single "failure," *Moment by Moment*—and that's a big difference in dollars and cents.

Working twelve to fourteen hours a day, Richard Gere literally immersed himself in the world of Julian Kay. Even off the set, he was wearing Julian's lizard-skin boots, designer jeans, and dark linen sports coat; in fact, he continued to wear the wardrobe for months after production ended. Gere has a habit of making his characters so real to himself that they haunt him for months after work has come to an end, as he waits for them to "wear off." This complete immersion in the role is one reason he doesn't like to have strangers, especially journalists, on the set. "It is an environment I like to be in control of. I don't like to have aliens there, new faces. They don't feed the work. And I don't like people around the set who know Richard. They'll start projecting Richard on me, and it ain't Richard there." Only through the exercise of this kind of tight control can Richard Gere allow his character to reveal himself in every way.

When Schrader initially conceived the film,

he intended to have almost no sex in it. "I had this idea of the gigolo as the well-dressed man, the man who wears a tie in Los Angeles, who is polite and knows his place, and who is selling something really kind of special, which is an attitude. I wanted to get away from the suntan-oiled chest and that kind of sleazy appeal." He and Gere thought that the true subject of the film was *surfaces*. Julian Kay should have the fantasy appeal of a daydream, a magazine ad hero, not the sweaty smell of a real body. But then Schrader realized he would have to include some sexuality in order to show his audience who Julian *really* is. After all, he is the man who asserts, "You want to know where I came from? I came from this bed," and "You can learn everything there is to know about me by fucking me."

The result of this rethinking was the exposure of a lot more of Richard Gere. He shows off that wonderful body in an exercise scene (it included the use of the soon-to-be-stylish gravity boots), and the camera lingers to let us feel the full effect. And he also has a couple of steamy love scenes, including one with Lauren Hutton that shows him in a state of full frontal nudity. That was a demand very few serious actors would have been willing to meet, but Gere did it with grace and poise. Schrader recalled, "Lauren was mortified at the thought of doing the love scene, and she covered up any part of her body that wasn't shown on camera. But Richard wanted the sex to be far more graphic than it was and he worked the whole day in the nude. I'd say Richard is very comfortable with his body."

Lauren Hutton paid her own moving tribute to the professional courage of her co-star. "There's a deep quality, a sensitivity beneath the tough, hoody veneer he puts on in *Gigolo* ... you can see it through his eyes. There's a real true sweetness and tenderness in Richard; he's very young and touching and vulnerable. The day I realized we were going to be friends was the day he had to stand naked in a room full of men and make that speech (about his God-given gift to women) over and over and over. That was a very brave thing to do ... and I was very touched. I was just lying there in that bed, listening and watching, and after a while, I found myself reacting to Richard not as Julian Kay but as Richard the man, and tears were streaming down my face, tears for all the pain an actor must go through."

Despite the strains of such scenes, making *American Gigolo* was a professionally rewarding experience for Richard Gere. As he explained, "This was my fifth major film, so I felt very much in control of the situation." He and Schrader worked well together, and grew very close in their shared viewpoint about the work they were creating. Gere said, "After the first few weeks, we didn't have to talk much at all because we knew exactly what we were doing. Paul and I had seen the same films. We knew stylistically how to do this. It was a shorthand." Since Richard is very interested in the process of filmmaking, he enjoyed being such an integral part of it all.

Schrader is generous in his praise of Richard Gere, both as an actor and as a screen presence: "If he has to come up for a big scene, he'll be up for it. On the other hand, he doesn't chew scenery. He knows when to be aggressive and when to be recessive. . . . I think he's got it all—a look, a style, a temperament, a talent. He blows the screen apart in this movie, I tell you."

All those concerned with *American Gigolo* had high hopes that this time Gere would come across as a strong enough screen reality to make the movie a big hit. Before its release, Richard took the risk of revealing his own daydreams about the movie's success. "I don't project what the movie will do for me. There are enough people around me who worry about things like that. But yeah, I give a shit. It would be fantastic if this movie did incredible business. I wouldn't have to worry about being third in line for a part I wanted to play. You see, it's not a question of who's the best actor. The corporation just says we'll make more money with this person. Knowing that, I play accordingly . . . within reason, of course."

As it turned out, the movie did more for Richard Gere the sex symbol than it did for Richard Gere the movie star. His love scenes, and his frontal nudity, attracted a lot of attention . . . well, how could you have expected it to be otherwise? And that attention overshadowed the other aspects of the film, about which critical opinion was divided. Everyone agreed the film looked good, as did Gere, but was there anything under that surface? Most people felt that in the end, Gere was unable to make Julian Kay a figure who touched the hearts of the audience.

Of course, it is only right to put some of the blame for this inadequacy firmly on the shoulders of the actor involved. But in all fairness, we should also remember that another major reason for the failure of Julian Kay to win the audience was surely the nature of the character himself. Julian was meant to be a shallow man, closed off from deep emotion, until the very end of the picture when he finally admits his need for the heroine, Michelle. So the very integrity of Gere's performance may have been one reason *American Gigolo* did not make him a real movie star. Since he did not "cheat" by trying to make Julian a more sympathetic and likable character than the script intended him to be, many viewers were repelled by the character—and blamed it on the actor.

Vincent Canby, in his review in *The New York Times*, expressed an understanding of Gere's dilemma. He said, "Richard Gere . . . has what is probably an impossible assignment. Julian Kay is someone of absolutely no visible charm or interest, and though Mr. Gere is a handsome, able, low-key actor, he brings no charm or interest to the role." He went on to add, "Then, too, the camera is not kind to him. It's not that he doesn't look fine, but that the camera seems unable to find any personality, like Dracula, whose image is unreflected by a mirror. Mr. Gere stands in front of a camera, but when the film is developed, the essential image has vanished." The *New Yorker*'s review stated, "Richard Gere is a considerable actor, given the proper kind of material, but in *American Gigolo* he has no place to go, literally and in our imagination."

Other reviewers were unfortunately less friendly. *People* was witty but cruel: "The heretofore gifted Gere . . . seems unable to act his way out of a Vuitton bag." *Newsweek* opined, "Gere tries. He looks good in and out of his Giorgio Armani suits. But he is a 'star' with a fatal lack of personality. Like a poem, a good screen actor shouldn't mean, but be. With Gere, you sense him searching for his character without ever embodying it." And David Denby, in

New York, ruminated, "As the chief luxury item, Richard Gere is thoroughly self-centered, which is probably right for the film. Gere is muscular but not heavy and blockish in fantasy-queen style; the sweetness in his dark eyes is set off by a large, bold street fighter's nose. Physically, the mixture of tenderness and roughness, strength and grace, is perfect, but here, as in his other movie roles, Gere never really develops a character. This actor lacks a strong sense of his identity. He does insolent self-assurance well, and boyish panic, but these are actor's turns—properties—and not the same thing as creating a fantasy large and generous enough to include the audience as participant. Even though Julian is supposed to be on top of his life, Gere doesn't convey much pleasure (as, say, Errol Flynn would have in the same role). Egotism in a young man can be most engaging, but Gere is too tight—he shuts us out."

When the discussion of *American Gigolo* was all over, Richard Gere seemed to be still standing in the very same place. Yes, we all agreed, he *was* sexy . . . and sales of posters showing a largely undraped Gere were brisk, as was the demand for similar shots in magazine articles. And sure, you have to agree that he knows how to act, as long as he has decent material and a good, supportive director. But we decided that he simply wasn't yet a STAR. He hadn't reached out to grab us. We might daydream about what we'd do if we could get our hands on that body, but we didn't incorporate his face, his *soul*, in our interior fantasy world. Richard Gere could show us his penis, he could even show us his pain, but he couldn't seem to show us his real self. And so, like him, we held ourselves aloof.

Chapter Nine

Applause for an Actor

It's the summer of 1979, and the shooting of *American Gigolo* is over. Richard Gere is enjoying a few weeks of well-deserved vacation. Well, maybe calling it a vacation is a bit misleading. First he went to Cannes, to attend the opening of *Days of Heaven* at the festival there. Then he went on to Rome, to meet with director Franco Zefferelli and talk about their planned production of *Hamlet*, to be staged in Los Angeles in the fall. Then Richard drifted on to India, Nepal, Thailand, and Bali. "I've always traveled for work. This was purely exploratory. I learned I don't have to live my life according to what other people expect."

When Richard Gere returned to New York, the circumstances of his life were still somewhat unsettled. He was for the time being living in the Sherry Netherland hotel, explaining, "I have no home. I have no things. I have no place to keep them. I just gave everything away. . . . A hotel is a good neutral place to maintain your character." He cleared off his calendar to give him a full year for the *Hamlet* production, commenting, "I don't look at doing Hamlet on the stage as taking time off from the thrust of my career. It's a challenge I feel I must meet." He was, of course, looking forward to his shot at every actor's dream role, as well as to working with the florid Zefferelli. Laurence Olivier was helping to make the cuts in Shakespeare's original (which would take more than four hours to enact), and the excellent supporting cast was already signed, included Roy Scheider, E. G. Marshall, Amy Irving, and Jean Simmons.

But Hamlet was not to be. The Center Theatre group, who was sponsoring the production, backed out. They gave as a reason the impossibility of keeping to the initial schedule; observers believed they were also alarmed at the size of the projected budget. Gere was disappointed but concluded philosophically, "I guess it was a dangerous thing to do at this stage of my career, but I'd rather get criticized now, after only five films, instead of later. They'll go for my throat, anyway."

Still, he yearned to return to the stage. He was certain that acting only to the unresponsive eye of the camera eventually depletes any performer; only a live audience can give something back to the actor. And he was attracted to the risk. He had the theory that "theater should be dangerous. I think it should be the opposite of sitting in front of a movie screen or a television—where you know that what you're seeing has already been filmed. In the theater, you should feel that you are involved with the play, and that you can have an effect on what's going to happen. You're as much a part of the experience as the actors on the stage. The extreme of this feeling is that maybe the actors are going to jump down from there and grab you by the throat."

Knowing that his client wanted a stage vehicle, Gere's agent, Ed Limato, was looking for scripts. He ran across one written by Martin Sherman, a playwright who was represented by the same agency. The play was called *Bent*, and it was about the Nazi treatment of homosexuals. It had already been produced in England, at the Royal Court Theatre, with the talented Ian McKellen in the leading role; in fact, it was still running. Would Richard be interested in starring in an American production? Gere said later, "There are pieces that cry out at you as you read them, and *Bent* was one of those. The people and the situation were immediately recognizable in human terms." The very next day, he met with Sherman and the director, Robert Allen Ackerman. He remembers, "We really had very little to talk about. They were so clear about what the play was and what its best intentions were; they were very clear about the fact that it was not a gay play. There were other overtones. And then the next day I said that I was prepared to do it. It was that quick."

Gere summarizes the plot of *Bent* as "one horror after another." The play opens with Max (the part played by Gere) and his lover, Rudy, at home in Berlin in the late thirties. They make the mistake of picking up a gay storm trooper, who is sleeping off his hangover on their sofa. Suddenly, the Nazis burst into their apartment and slit the throat of the storm trooper. Max and Rudy escape, but not for long; soon they are picked up and loaded into a boxcar headed for Dachau. Forewarned that gays are treated even worse than Jews, Max denies that he is homosexual and, to save himself, even participates in killing Rudy. At the climax of this scene, he again proves his "manhood" by having intercourse with a dead thirteen-year-old girl. This wins him the right to wear the yellow Star of David of the Jews, rather than the pink triangle of the homosexuals.

But in the second act, Max becomes human.

He falls in love with a fellow prisoner Horst. In perhaps the most memorable scene in the play, they consummate an act of love, complete with orgasm, by talking to one another, fully dressed, three feet apart. Eventually, the camp guards discover their attachment, and they respond by killing the ailing Horst before Max's eyes. In a quick climax, Max rips the pink triangle off the body of his lover and puts it on his own uniform, then immolates himself on the electric fence.

Not exactly what you'd call an upbeat play. Not likely to appeal to the tourists, the couples from New Jersey who have come for a gala night on the town. Not a very glamorous role for a movie star, either, playing a concentration camp inmate with a shaved head. Worse yet, playing a *homosexual*. Audiences would think it meant ... would think he must be ... Well, naturally, they would identify him as ... There were plenty of people who told Richard Gere he was going to destroy his career by starring in *Bent*.

But he refused to be deterred by this well-meant advice. He said firmly, "Yes, I'm gay ... when I'm on that stage. If the role required me to suck off Horst, I'd do it. But I didn't consider taking the part a bold move. I'd been thinking for quite a while about getting back under that theatrical proscenium arch, and this was the best play I'd read in years. It has so many layers to it. It's about the nature of love, about accepting yourself and other people for what they are. It's ultimately life-affirming."

With his usual thoroughness, Richard Gere began to prepare for playing the part of Max. He read a number of books about the realities of life in a concentration camp, "books that would tear your heart out," and was especially struck by Bruno Bettelheim's *The Informed Heart*, which advanced the thesis that survival in a concentration camp, much like survival as a whole and functioning person in the ordinary world, depended on being able to maintain and express one's personality. In the early fall, when Gere had to go to Rome to accept his Golden David award for his performance in *Days of Heaven*, he took the opportunity to make an excursion to Dachau. "You feel the texture of the place when you get near it. There's misery— the texture of misery. It's a frightening place. The camp is almost all there. The barracks have been burned down, but the foundations are there. You see the administration building, the crematorium, the camp, the wire around the fence, the original signs. It's overpowering. There are ghosts hanging about."

On that same trip, he also stopped in Munich, to look for remnants of the pre-war gay scene in Germany, and was struck by the hostile and violent mood of its current homosexual community. Back in California for some post-production work on *American Gigolo*, he went to talk to the well-known writer Christopher Isherwood, who had been a part of the Berlin group that Sherman wrote about. Bit by bit, he began to build up the character of Max. The only thing he didn't do was to go see the London production of *Bent* and the much-acclaimed performance of McKellen in the role of Max. "I wanted to come to the part in my own way."

The further Richard Gere got into the character of Max, the more he began to see that Max was really very much like Julian Kay. Gere commented, "I think the central human dilemma is being able to say, 'Yes, this is who I am ... with no bullshit attached. Accept me, please.' And also saying, 'Yes, I will accept your love and will take responsibility.' When we can do that, we're happy. When we can't, we're living outside somehow. It isn't just gays, it's all of us. We carry around this weight, which is the metaphor of the second act. We carry around this weight without even being able to look at each other and being able to stop and say, 'I love you.' The final line of the play is 'I love you.' What's wrong with that?"

But as much as Gere loved the play, enacting the role of Max night after night was a draining experience. It was physically tiring. He was on stage nearly every minute of the play; moreover, during much of the long second act, he was carrying twenty-pound rocks back and forth across the stage. (The actors had agreed to use real ones, instead of papier-mâché replicas, so the audience could hear the crash as they dropped, and see the actors work up a genuine sweat.) But even more significant was the emotional strain. Gere explained: "The gamut of emotions in the play . . . I've never had a part like it. You can't imagine what it's like to be shattered every night. Like when I break through my own selfish defense and gently make love to Horst when he's so sick, because I need him, too. That's a beautiful moment. Then the guards say, 'Watch. *Watch.*' Then they kill him. Eight times a week I'm destroyed."

Gere did what he could to protect himself against the emotional drain. He refused to see people immediately before and after each performance, and for the most part, he lived extremely quietly, saving all of his energy for the stage. Yet friends remember that he lost weight steadily, and seemed almost literally haunted by the ghosts of Dachau. Director Ackerman felt that the demands of the part kept Gere in a state of depression for the eight-month run of the play.

That made Gere's willingness to work so hard all the more admirable. Says Ackerman, "He's an incredibly hard worker. There was nothing

he wasn't willing to try; he was always available,
never showed any temperament. He could have
just spent two hours lifting rocks, and if he
overheard some actor saying something about
missing a sequence, Richard would immediately offer to do it. He's so focused, so concentrated, so extraordinarily dedicated." He added
more compliments: "Richard is one of the most
intelligent actors I ever worked with; there's
nothing he won't reveal to an audience." (In
this case, he's talking about *emotions!*) The
author had similarly warm feelings about the
actor who brought Max to life. Martin Sherman
said, "I can't tell you how good Richard is.
Incredible levels, endless depth, endless colors.
He is brilliantly alive on stage."

For once, the critics agreed with Gere's co-
workers. When the play opened on December
2, 1979, his reviews were generally very good.
Time commended his "arresting performance"
and added, "Throughout the play, Gere han-
dles the shadings of emotion superbly, especially in the scene in which he and David Dukes
(Horst) stand several feet apart, not facing each
other, and go through an explicit verbal depic-
tion of oral sex all the way to its climax." Clive
Barnes said, "Gere is enormously gifted, and
although he overdoes his initial hangover, many
of the later scenes reveal an impressively raw
passion." Gere was also called "extremely

effective" and "a courageous actor, willing to take risks and possessed of the emotional resources to see them through." Even reviewers who compared Gere to Ian McKellen had to agree that the American actor did not suffer from the comparison.

No doubt Richard Gere enjoyed all the praise from the critics, but what gratified him even more than the reviews was the response by the live audience. "I get letters that are incredible. A lot of them are from gay people thanking me for doing the show. Even more gratifying are the letters from middle class people—priests, lawyers, housewives—who just never considered the gay question before. . . . The play humanizes the situation and makes the central problem just as personal to straight people as to a homosexual. It really comes down to being faced with this question of 'My God, all I want is to be loved and to love.' And people see it so clearly and so powerfully when they come out of this play. I've had letters from people telling me they'll be in their car on the way home from the show and they'll burst into tears. Or they'll turn their light out at night and they'll hear their mate sobbing. And I think that's wonderful."

But perhaps the response that meant the very most to Richard Gere personally came from his brother, who saw *Bent* several times. "After one of the shows he told me, 'I really like the Richard Gere I see now. You're in a totally different place than the last time I saw you.' That was one of the nicest things anybody could have said to me."

Chapter Ten

Coming to Terms with Success

Bent provided a significant turning point in Richard Gere's professional life and not simply because of the good reviews. They were nice to have, but Broadway success means pitifully little in Hollywood's eyes. And not for the financial rewards of an eight-month run: Even in smash hits, Broadway salaries can't begin to compare with those of Hollywood. No, the real reason ran deeper. *Bent* meant a lot to Richard Gere because his success in the play proved he could take risks and win. He didn't have to be cast in Hollywood's inflexible mold for leading men but could choose his own eclectic way. *And* still keep his fans, his image, his stardom.

Paul Schrader noticed concrete evidence of this victory when he visited Gere backstage

during the run of *Bent*. "The demographics of
the stage door have changed since the opening
of *Gigolo*," he decided. "There's a small but
extraordinarily hardy contingent of young girls
who weren't there previously. And they don't
seem to mind in the least when Richard comes
out looking like a Dachau victim instead of the
luscious fruit of Hollywood, the glamorous
Southern California fantasy they've come to see."
In other words, his fans were quite willing—
perhaps even eager—to accept both sides of
Richard Gere: the serious actor and the sex
symbol.

To Richard Gere himself, the two sides had
once seemed to be locked in mortal combat.
But now he, too, was able to reconcile the
differences. "Isn't it ridiculous," he said to an
interviewer while he was appearing in *Bent*,
"that I look sexy in *American Gigolo*? I laughed
out loud when I saw the print of it. I mean,
each night I put on my makeup and I look like
a lobotomy victim. Then I see what I looked
like eight months ago. You can see the absurdity of appearance."

The fact that the two characters, Max and
Julian Kay, were so much alike under their
contrasting exteriors made the point even sharp-
er. It was very liberating for Gere to realize
that he could play a character who looks terrible,
who denies his friendship in order to save his
skin, who participates in killing his friend and

117

copulates with a dead child—and still make that character (and himself) not just acceptable, but a sort of hero to the audience by the end of the evening. At last, Gere, like Max and Julian, felt that he was being accepted for himself.

Playing Max freed Richard Gere in another way, too. His success as an actor had always come from his ability to immerse himself totally in his role, virtually to *become* his character. But that kind of complete identification has its price: The actor begins to wonder if he has any personality of his own or whether it's been overpowered by the character he plays. Gere had expressed a fear of this possibility: "You have to be careful. They'll [the characters] come knocking on your door. They'll want to come out. . . . We all fantasize about who we are and who we want to be. But I actually do them physically. So it's a little dangerous when you're playing with that." Because of such a fear, Max was obviously a threatening role; not only was it powerfully written, but also Gere had to play it day after day, week after week, month after month. It certainly *did* have an effect on him, both physically and mentally. But it also proved beyond a doubt that Richard Gere the actor was stronger than any of his characters. He concluded thankfully, "I learn so much through these people I play, no doubt about it. After you play so many roles, you start to feel the reincarnation aspects of reality, the multipersonality aspects of a consciousness. They're all right there, bubbling in this core, which is where the real creativity comes from. I used to be afraid of that, jumping in and not being able to get out. But the more you play around with it, the more you realize how fluid it is, and you don't have to be locked into it."

The beneficial effects of playing the part of Max were heightened by the release soon afterward of *American Gigolo*. Although the critics were not entirely satisfied with Gere's performance as Julian Kay, the film did a brisk business at the box office, fanned by the flames of publicity about Richard's sexy appeal. The film grossed more in its first week of release than any of Gere's other starring vehicles did in their entire lifespan—over $9 million. He was elated by this development: "Just the other day, Paul and I were saying we must find some other way to make a living, running guns to Afghanistan, maybe. Now people who wouldn't take our phone calls a week ago are calling us." Gere knew that the sudden spate of phone calls meant that he had just been given more power over the course of his own career, more choices of better roles. At the same time, he retained a healthy skepticism about the callers' motives. "This business is a roller-coaster ride. Once you get on, you can't get off, and there are a lot of peaks and valleys. When you hit the valley, the hustlers and vampires like to probe the kinks way down at the bottom. But as soon as you make a buck, they show up again, friendly as can be."

Riding on the crest of the box-office success of *American Gigolo* and the critical acclaim of *Bent*, Richard Gere found it was time in his personal life for new beginnings. He used part of his earnings from these two projects to buy a penthouse apartment in a handsome old Greenwich Village co-op, paying, it is rumored, about half a million dollars for it. That apartment is still his home today. Although Richard is wary about letting tattletale reporters glimpse his private retreat, one or two have managed to penetrate his defenses and get a look at the place. They describe a large, light living room, with gleaming floors of old-fashioned wide boards, partially covered by Oriental rugs. The furniture is a relaxed mix of American antiques and a few contemporary pieces. The focal point of the room is a grand piano, which bespeaks the fact that Richard's interest in music continues to play an important part in his life. "When I play the piano, I eventually work up to a frenzy; it's very calming. Although I read music for the other instruments, for the piano it's whatever comes out—some of it sounds classical, some sounds popular." But he adds firmly, "Music is just *me*, I enjoy it. It's the only private thing I've got left. I doubt if I would ever do a big media number, making records and all that hype. No way. I don't think I could handle it."

Music is only one of the forms of mental relaxation that Richard Gere has devised for himself against the calm background of his penthouse refuge. Another is the regular practice of his tai chi chu'an exercises. They come from an ancient Chinese martial system and require slow, precise, but powerful movements. Rhythmic breathing is an important element in these energizing exercises, and Richard finds they help him both concentrate and relax. They are one of the ways he eases the tension between the need for control and the lack of control in his life.

Like the character he played in *American Gigolo*, Richard Gere also makes room in his apartment for the dumbbells and barbells he uses in his daily fitness workouts. He views his body matter-of-factly, as one of the tools of his actor's art, and to him it seems only sensible to keep it in the best possible condition. "I have muscles, so I use them," he says unapologetically, "just as I have a brain and I try to use it." One interviewer asked him rather pointedly what he would do when the inevitable effects of time mar the perfection of the body he uses to such good advantage. His answer reminds us that Richard was once a philosophy major: "I assume that everything on earth is in a state of transition. When circumstances change for me,

I hope to be involved in things for which I'm suited ... such as life." Meanwhile, he will continue to keep all of his tools in good working order.

By the time Richard Gere left the cast of *Bent*, in the summer of 1980, people who knew him well all agreed that he seemed calmer, more relaxed, and especially more at ease with his reputation and his fame. Many of them suspected that one reason underlying this transformation was his new relationship with Sylvia Martins. Of course, he had not lacked for companionship since his break with Penelope Milford, dating, among others, actress Barbara Carrera, but nothing seemed to be serious ... until Sylvia came along. According to a frequently repeated story (which may be legend rather than fact), she began to telephone him regularly when he returned to New York after the completion of *Yanks*, saying only, "I'm Sylvia from Brazil and I'd like to meet you." At last he was able to put a face to this mysterious voice when one evening at Elaine's, a New York restaurant that serves as a gathering spot for creative types, she boldly marched up to his table and introduced herself. In no time at all, they were seeing each other regularly, and after a while, Sylvia moved into his apartment.

Sylvia Martins is an attractive and petite brunette, several years younger than Richard. She has done some modeling (her picture has been on the cover of the Brazilian edition of Vogue), and she is currently making a name for herself as a painter. Although she often flies back to Rio for long visits with her family when the weather turns cold, she has been a steadying influence in Richard's life. One friend described her by saying, "She's so open and friendly, she has a very calming effect on Richard." He himself has always recognized the importance of surrounding himself with people who really care about what's best for him. "If I don't want people in my life, they're not there. All the people in my life are serious, dedicated people."

These changes in Richard Gere's personal life began to be reflected in his professional life as well. He didn't take things quite so hard as he used to, didn't feel so angry about the unfairness and stupidity he necessarily encountered in his daily existence. He revealed, "I don't feel as threatened by publicity as I used to. I don't feel that immediate violation of my privacy. . . . Most interviewers characterize themselves in what they write more than the subject they're writing about, anyway. Out of it all, I'm learning how to evaluate my own worth. Directors I thought were gods are treating me like an equal for the first time in my life. And for the first time in my life, I'm beginning to realize it is finally possible to be an equal." Another sign of his lightening mood was the fact that he began to think about the possibility of doing comedy. In short, he was learning to relish the absurdity of life, just like some of the directors he most admired.

As the months went by, Richard Gere became more and more open to the wide range of choices that were now available to him, and he took some time to reflect on them and to savor the situation. Paul Schrader sketched out some of Gere's options at this point: "Richard has a number of careers branching out in front of him. He has the rare opportunity to choose one of several personae: the traditional leading man, the introspective actor of the tormented-soul school, a model or icon, or a Broadway actor. His appeal to women is enormous—he's handsome enough to be male model, and he's probably the only one of our serious young actors you could say that about. Yet there's a personality, a masculine *credibility*, behind his looks that make him very special. The limit to his success as an actor is the degree he plays to his looks or plays against them. I'm not sure what he wants to be, and I'm not sure he's sure."

It seems that Gere's own preference is not to have to choose any one restricting path but to embrace all the possibilities that are available to him. He says, "I feel good about all of it. I'm doing things that excite me, interest me, help me grow both personally and professionally. . . . I now see my career in terms of a wider spectrum. Certain aspects about the profession don't piss me off the way they used to." His conclusion is a satisfying one: "I guess I've managed to escape most of the madness."

Chapter Eleven
The Big Film

After the release of *American Gigolo* in early 1981, one studio executive summed up Hollywood's attitude toward Richard Gere: "He's so good, a producer is ready to gamble—instantly. Everybody in the business knows that it's just a matter of time, a matter of the right role, the right director, the right combination for it all to come together."

And it finally did come together, just as he predicted. The role was Zack Mayo; the picture was *An Officer and a Gentleman*. It was another Paramount production (the man in charge this time was Martin Elfand). The film started out with a script written by Douglas Day Stewart, who was also responsible for the screenplay of the hit *Blue Lagoon*. The story Stewart sketched out may have lacked subtlety, but it definitely carried a big emotional punch. Stewart's hero was a young man with a chip on his shoulder, the son of a hard-drinking, womanizing sailor and a mother who committed suicide after her husband deserted her. From this difficult childhood, Zack has grown into a man with a hard shell—a selfish loner who is afraid to love or trust anyone else, but who is determined to make something of himself. As the first step in his program to turn himself into "an officer and a gentleman," he manages to get accepted to the Navy's Officer Candidate School.

The real focus of *An Officer and a Gentleman* is what happens to Zack Mayo while he is attending OCS, an environment the screenwriter knew well, since he, too, had once been a trainee in such a place. The film surrounds him with a cast of stereotypes: the mean drill instructor, the naively honest friend, the girl who unselfishly offers him the love he is afraid to accept, the gold digger who is trying to trick another trainee into marriage, the female trainee who finally wins acceptance as a buddy. The film then pulls off the unexpected feat of making these clichés create real emotions for the audience.

The leading role of Zack Mayo was practically tailor-made for Richard Gere. Zack is another character, like Julian and Max, who doesn't know how to accept (or offer) real love. The underlying drama of *An Officer and a Gentleman* is the transformation of Zack as he finally understands that he must reveal his weaknesses and risk the possibility of pain and rejection if he is to obtain the trust and love that all humans need to survive psychologically. What makes Zack more attractive than Gere's previous roles is that he learns this lesson earlier in life (and, of course, earlier in the film), and he also embraces its truth more wholeheartedly. Thus the audience gets a chance to see and enjoy the man he becomes. *Newsweek* analyzed the appeal of this "before and after" aspect of the movie: "It was a perfect merger of movie iconographies and of women's conflicting fantasies that wanted their men at once wild and civilized. . . . In *An Officer and a Gentleman*, Gere acts out both fantasies. Zack the wild one (who wears a tattoo, rides a motorcycle, and lives in a dive with his whore-mongering father) becomes Zack the executive (who accepts discipline, wears a shiny white suit, and isn't afraid to love). Marlon Brando becomes Gary Cooper, and Richard Gere becomes a star whom both men and women can respond to."

The director Paramount tapped for the film was Taylor Hackford, who had previously directed *The Idolmaker*. His hallmark was quick action and a real appreciation of the energies and ambitions of youth. Hackford had no qualms about getting some exciting action sequences on film, but he was concerned about other aspects of the movie's appeal. He says he was always completely convinced that Richard Gere the actor had the potential to make Zack Mayo the character touch the hearts of a mass movie audience. But he was aware that there might be some problems in getting that performance on the screen. "I felt that Richard had this immense, complex stuff inside, and I'd like to deal with it and reveal some. I had always felt Richard had a terrific presence onscreen, but I'd oftentimes felt a kind of veneer there, that he didn't let you in. And when I talked with him, we had to be very honest with one another, and I said what I would hope to do was try to get past that."

This question of a veneer—or as many put it, a barrier—between Richard Gere and his audience was one that had been frequently raised in the past, and many people were convinced that it was the only reason he had not yet become a superstar. Critics often complained of his distance, his seeming lack of rapport with the camera/audience; as one phrasemaker put it, even in his best performances, "he remained a gleaming, self-contained, and self-regarding vessel." Stephen Harvey, writing in 1980, expressed these reservations more harshly: "I wonder whether an actor who appears so much more comfortable exuding narcissism than menschness could ever really become a popular favorite—particularly when this is conveyed with so little humor, much less a trace of self-deprecation. If Gere possessed a looser, more generous-spirited screen personality, nobody would bother quibbling over the apparent limitations of a movie actor-star's technique. . . ." Even *Teen* magazine jumped on the bandwagon and criticized one of its readers' favorite sex symbols: "Judging Richard by his role [in *American Gigolo*], audiences found him to be both fascinating and sexy, yet uncomfortably aloof. They perceived him as intriguing rather than likeable. By choosing to play a character who was neither endearing nor vulnerable, he won the audience's admiration but not their affection."

But director and star quickly agreed about the goal of capturing those qualities of warmth and vulnerability that make a true star on the screen. They felt all it would take was a lot of hard work. *An Officer and a Gentleman* was another demanding film for Richard Gere. Physically, it certainly required that he be in peak condition. Not only would he once again have to expose nearly every square inch of his body in love scenes, but also he had to carry off a number of action scenes. He had to go through the ordinary calisthenics of the trainee, a somewhat wearing experience. There was also a scene that required scrambling repeatedly over a rigorous obstacle course. Then he had to learn some karate and kick-fighting moves for two different scenes; one in which he fights off some jeering townies and another, longer, scene in which he finally challenges the drill instructor (superbly played by Lou Gossett, Jr.) to all-out combat.

But far and away the most difficult scene Gere had to prepare for was the crucial one in which the drill instructor, trying to force Zack to quit OCS, first disciplines him with an inhuman number of sit-ups, push-ups and leg lifts, and then needles him as he approaches the physical and emotional breaking point. The climax of the scene comes when an exhausted Zack finally reveals his desperation and vulnerability as the drill instructor threatens to kick him out of the training program. Panicked into facing his naked need, Zack shouts, "Don't do it! I got no place to go!" Critic Janet Maslin, of *The New York Times,* remarked about this scene, "If the audience doesn't believe this, the movie is lost." She went on to add approvingly, "Mr. Gere makes it utterly real."

Director Hackford later gave us a behind-the-scenes look at just how real this scene became for Richard Gere. Hackford says it was shot in one long weekend of "virtual torture," and that it was shot in its continuity sequence, with Gere going step-by-step through the exhausting physical and emotional stresses that lead up to Zack's final abandonment of his tough-guy pose. Only an extremely disciplined—and very talented—actor could pull off such a feat, taking the physical abuse while continuing to function as a performer. And Hackford adds one last detail about the filming that encapsulates Gere's tremendous professionalism. When the actor climbed painfully down from the concrete bunker after the scene had reached its emotional climax, Hackford noticed that the back of his shirt was wet with blood. "He'd been stretched out there doing leg lifts with a nasty abscess on his back. Never mentioned it to me."

Behavior like that is what endears stars to directors, so you can believe it didn't take long for Taylor Hackford to become a real fan of Richard Gere. He was particularly impressed by what he saw as Gere's growth as an actor since he had appeared in his last movie, *American Gigolo*. Hackford thought his experience acting in *Bent* might be a large part of the reason for his improvement. "The degradation of that role worked against that kind of pretty-boy image that his previous roles had exemplified." Hackford went on to reflect about Gere the man: "With the press, he's got this heavy defensiveness that people translate into arrogance. But mostly it is shyness. With people he does let in—we're friends now—he's a perfectly warm, reasonable person."

Perhaps it was Hackford's personal admiration for Gere that helped him succeed in revealing more of the actor's own warmth and charm on the screen at last. This success was especially noticeable (and much appreciated by the audiences) in Gere's love scenes with his leading lady, Debra Winger. Now, it's not as if fans had never before noticed that Richard Gere is sexy . . . after all, we didn't have our eyes closed when he unveiled that wonderful body in *American Gigolo*, or when he performed that wild, erotic dance in *Looking for Mr. Goodbar*, or when he was in bed with his girl friend in *Yanks*. But somehow those scenes, although they certainly portrayed the heat of passion, lacked the more subtle warmth of real feeling. They made us uncomfortably aware of a kind of self-containment that at worst bordered on narcissism and at best made audiences feel shut out from the actor/character's feelings. But in *An Officer and a Gentleman*, Gere was more than sexy: He was an emotional turn-on as well as a physical one. This gave the bedroom scenes real power. In fact, they were so real that they made couples in the audience instinctively reach out to touch one another, and made people who saw it alone yearn for the presence of that special someone. But not just *anyone*, you understand; Tony Lopanto may have made us think about trying to pick up an exciting one-night stand, but Zack Mayo made us hungry for some emotional intimacy bound up with that physical satisfaction.

Of course, part of the credit for the success of the love story in *An Officer and a Gentleman* must go to the other half of the screen romance, Debra Winger. Her role of Paula Pokrifki, the factory worker who finds her own happy ending quite literally being carried off in the arms of Zack Mayo, was her third major film in a single year. In her first, she played the wife of John Travolta in *Urban Cowboy* (a film, it may be recalled, that Gere once had his own eye on). Her scene riding the mechanical bull was unforgettable, and it led to her being cast in *Cannery Row*, the screen adaptation of the Steinbeck novel. She played a young prostitute, opposite another leading heartthrob, Nick Nolte. The film was a bomb, but critics all agreed that the fault definitely was not Winger's. So she went on to play Paula, making love on the screen with another of America's sexiest leading men. She won rave reviews for her performance, including an Oscar nomination, and although she didn't upstage Richard Gere, she certainly held her own against his star magnetism. "Damp hair askew, her face puffy with desire, Debra Winger, sitting astride Gere, is perhaps the most openly erotic actress ever to appear in mainstream Hollywood movies," said David Denby of *New York*. *Newsweek*'s critic called her "one of those rare actresses who seems to open herself totally to the camera: Every moment is raw, honest, freshly discovered." Pauline Kael's was the most enthusiastic review. "Paula's tough-chick little-girl insolence plays off the avid look in her eyes that tells you she longs to make human contact—she's daring you to trust her. And what may be the world's most expressive upper lip tells you that she's hungrily sensual; when she's trying to conceal her raw feelings, her hoarse voice, with its precarious pitch, gives her away."

If Richard Gere was indebted to Debra Winger for helping him make Zack Mayo a truly romantic hero, he owed just as much to Lou Gossett for giving Zack a worthy mentor/opponent. The mastery of Gossett's performance was unmistakable. As *New York*'s David Denby put it, "As Gossett launches into his first tirade, enunciating the words with icy clarity and disdain, you know that the performance is a classic. . . ." Pauline Kael commented wittily that "Gossett is as definite and beyond question as Barbara Woodhouse is when she's giving orders to dog owners," and went on to conclude, "At times he suggests a member of a superior race." Ultimately, Hollywood confirmed the validity of all this praise from reviewers by giving him the Oscar for Best Supporting Actor.

Despite the accolades for supporting players, there was never any question about the fact that *An Officer and a Gentleman* was Richard Gere's movie. Although many reviewers felt compelled to put down the movie for its old-fashioned attitude toward women and marriage, and its copious use of stereotype characters, about the star they were generally laudatory. *Horizon* said, "You'll want to stand up and cheer as the American Gigolo becomes the American Actor." Janet Maslin, in *The New York Times*, asserted, "Gere has never been this affecting before; there's an urgency to his performance, some of it visibly induced by the hard physical work of the basic-training sequences, that cuts right through his manner of detachment." *People*, in one of those back-handed compliments that leaves a sting, said, "Gere, usually an actor of catatonic drabness, delivers his first passionate screen performance." *Newsweek* refrained from raking up old criticisms and confined itself to saying simply, "Gere gives his best, least-mannered performance, rarely drifting out of character." Even Pauline Kael, one of Gere's harshest critics, recognized the improvement: "Gere still has a blank look too often, but he has got past the facile-mannered performances in which he sounded like three or four fifties stars; you can see an honest effort to go inside the character of Zack and inhabit it, and the picture seems tailor-made for him."

No performer is immune to the pleasure of good reviews, but in this instance Richard Gere was probably much more thrilled by the box-office business than he was by the critical approval. *An Officer and a Gentleman* was released in the late summer of 1982, and by the end of the year, it was the second biggest film in gross receipts, beaten only by *E.T.* Its ultimate gross in its theatrical release topped $125 million, making it one of the real biggies. Its sale of television rights brought in another whopping sum, and retailers report that the videocassette version of the film continues to rank in the top five on their sales charts. It all adds up to the kind of big bucks the dealmakers in Hollywood and New York love to hear about. And this time, Richard Gere got all the credit. At last he was standing tall in the front ranks of the truly bankable leading men. From now on, his interest in a project would be enough to turn it into a reality.

The power that Richard Gere wanted was finally in his grasp.

Chapter Twelve

Using the Power

By the fall of 1982, it was clear that *An Officer and a Gentleman* was going to be a box-office smash. At last, Richard Gere had the dollars-and-cents success he needed to put him in a position of genuine power in the film industry. He had finally become a truly bankable star.

And that meant he could do just about anything he wanted to do.

It was the situation Gere had been working to achieve for more than ten years, and you can bet he had some ideas about what he wanted to do next. His goals were admittedly iconoclastic. "If I'm to become a public figure, I will not perpetuate lies. I want to break away from accepted patterns, values that we've learned through the marketing of a product." But he

was willing to recognize the obligations his
new power carried with it. "I feel responsible
for the message of the movie and the motives
of the filmmakers. And people might be coming to see a film because my name is on it.
That's a major responsibility."

Interestingly, it seemed that Richard Gere's
choice of a medium, now that he could choose
anything he wanted, was to be film rather than
live theater. He had in the past spoken rather
passionately about the limitations of acting for
the camera rather than for a live audience.
"Moviemaking is like jerking off. You don't get
energy back. Audiences are energy. If you don't
share your experience with them, it's like never
really coming. Even in *Habeas Corpus*, on
Broadway, where I had a small role, I'd feel the
give and take. Without it, I get cross, irritable.
Because the audience tells me if I'm good. On
film, it's give and take with a machine." He
summed up the central deficiency of movie
acting: "You are focusing your energy into the
camera lens—that piece of glass."

But, despite his reservations, Gere recognized
that film had significant advantages as a creative medium. One of these advantages, of
course, is the reality of its enormous influence.
Even a long-running play is never seen by a
very large number of people, whereas a successful movie is seen by millions. Moreover, its
characters and ideas may become part of the

nation's—perhaps even the world's—cultural heritage. The way we define good and evil, our concepts of success and failure, our ideals of family life, romance, relationships between men and women: They are all defined in part by the movies we see. For example, the screen persona of John Wayne created a male role model for a whole generation of American men; Marilyn Monroe did the same thing for the young women of the fifties. The films of Katharine Hepburn taught us that independent woman *can* be attractive; more recently, Woody Allen made it clear that even hopeless wimps can be lovable. Gere's own *An Officer and a Gentleman* both expressed and helped to create the notion that good old-fashioned romance was back in style. The filmmaker has immense power to shape the dreams and beliefs of large numbers of people.

The second advantage of film as a medium is its potential for artistic expression. Although every film is a collaborative effort, it can nevertheless be carefully shaped to express a single point of view or an aesthetic. And the medium's technical resources give the filmmaker virtually limitless freedom to say, and show, whatever he wants to. On film, all things are possible, all visions can be realized; it only takes time and patience—and the financial resources. You can revisit the past, visualize the future, turn imaginary characters into tangible form. You can move seamlessly from one place to the next, or from one point of view to another.

These were some of the reasons that Richard Gere committed himself to a future in film. He believed he could succeed in combining artistic validity with commercial acceptance. "Artists with high artistic standards," he says, "continually have to fight for what they feel is good. The studios are not necessarily opposed to quality, but you—the actor, director, or writer—have to help them understand how quality fits their economic needs." After years of observing the Hollywood scene, he had concluded that, "The smart artists in the film business buffer themselves from the corporate structures so that they have minimum interference," and obviously, he hoped to achieve just such a happy compromise. Audaciously, he intended to use the studio's resources to teach audiences to expect something better than the standard studio product. "I think people can be educated away from negative cheap-thrill movies to great movies . . . I don't think it's wishful thinking. I really believe it's just a matter of time before people get tired of being lied to by their television sets and the phony movies and find satisfaction in a deeper level of experience. I believe in mental evolution—for myself and for everybody."

It was Richard Gere's ambition to become more involved with the creative end of filmmaking. He had been preparing himself. "When I'm not in a scene, I don't fool around. I'm looking through the camera to watch each shot being assembled. I've learned how to diffuse light, which lenses to use to get different effects. There are all sorts of new territories I want to explore. You can't do that if you spend your time building a movie-star persona." He had considered the possibility of writing a screenplay himself but finally concluded, "I just have no time. There are a couple that I took to their natural conclusion and decided that they weren't going to get done. I didn't like them. And there are some that are kicking around that still have value to me. They may get done." But even with the limitations on his time, he felt he could make a contribution to the scripts of the movies in which he would star. He could suggest dialogue, even entire scenes, that were appropriate to his character, and thus function as a full partner in the creation of the character and the action.

Richard Gere was also drawn to the possibility of directing films. "Certainly I have my own idea of how things should be done. . . . It's definitely an impulse." But, he recognized, "I may not have the temperament for it. I don't like dealing with a lot of other people." Moreover, he was positive that he couldn't pull off the feat of directing a movie in which he was also starring: "When you're acting, you're just so fucked up the whole time that you're very short with the people who are pulling on you.''

After considering all his options, Gere concluded that the best way for him to exercise his newfound power was to continue with what had made him successful—his career as an actor. But in the future, things would be different. He could select his own parts, no longer having to take whatever turned up in order to work. He could initiate his own projects when he found a concept or script that appealed to him. He could use his leverage to influence the studio's other choices, such as co-stars, directors, and technicians. How pleasant to have the shoe at last on the other foot! With the major studios now needing Gere's box-office potential more than he needed any particular job, he could dictate the conditions under which he would—or would not—work. Never a prima donna, he would use his status as a bankable star not to get a bigger dressing room or a snazzier wardrobe or salaries for an entourage, but to get the things the film itself needed to make it the best possible end product. Richard Gere was no longer "just" an actor. He was now a Star.

But of course his craft *was* acting, and many people who had followed his career agreed that he was at last an actor at the top of his form. He'd always had the raw talent; and now, with years of experience, he had also acquired the necessary technique. His confident sense of mas-

tery was evident in the increased ease of his
screen performances. He had once said that
". . . the creative high is as close as many of us
get to God," and although the Richard Gere
of 1982 found that statement a bit embarrassing in its ingenuousness, he still felt that actors were lucky in their choice of profession.
Through acting, they get the chance to experience those rare creative moments when something new happens, something no one foresaw
or expected, "the surprise that comes when
you get into unknown territories." He relished
the notion that in certain challenging scenes,
Zack Mayo's psychological surrender to the drill
instructor in *An Officer and a Gentleman,* "You
may get into a scene like that and you may
know where you're pointing, but you don't know
where you're gonna end up. . . . Certainly, acting can be a very scary place."

Richard Gere had his own ideas about how
good acting happens. "You let certain aspects
of your personality go away somewhere, and
this void is left behind. Hopefully, you're meanwhile coaxing what you need to play the character from emotions and mysterious things
inside you—things that never really change."
Beyond the craft, of course, he knew that acting was a highly creative form of self-expression
(with an emphasis on the *self*). "Probably what
makes you want to be an actor to begin with
. . . is that you have felt things and you want to

express them in some way. And through art you find a metaphor to deal with something you've felt, whether it was conscious or totally unconscious. Expressing it in metaphorical terms purifies you in some way."

Like all truly talented actors, Richard Gere was never satisfied that what he finally saw on the screen was precisely what he had intended to project. As time went by, though, he learned to live with the gap between the performance in an actor's head and the one that appears on the screen. He commented ruefully, "It's difficult to see yourself. It's easier a year after the fact, when it's released, because you're in such a different feeling by then and you've usually done a few things since. You're a little easier on yourself. . . . You can never hit as high as you wanted to go. Never. Immediately after you do it, you're very aware of what you were trying to do. A year later, you forget exactly what you were trying to do, and you're more surprised by what you actually did get."

The success of *An Officer and a Gentleman* gave Richard Gere the power to choose the roles he wanted. But what were his criteria for choice? He admitted that his method of close personal identification with his character—of virtually creating the character out of bits and pieces of Richard Gere—was an important factor: "They're all Richard Gere; they couldn't be anyone else. And the root character of Richard

Gere changes in the process. Of course, there are similarities, drive-wise and core-wise, between some of the characters I play. That's probably why I've ended up playing them."

Gere's agent, Ed Limato, had some further thoughts on the subject. "I try to lead him to some middle ground between the altogether artistic and the commercial. Even so, he's what we call a director's actor, which is to say he usually goes over the script with the director before he makes a choice." Among the directors Gere hopes to be able to work with at some point in his career are Europeans Herzog, Antonioni, Costa-Gavras, and Wenders; among American directors, his choices are Coppola, Scorsese, and Hal Ashby.

But there was another, more subtle, factor at work when Richard Gere selected his roles, and with his usual bent for analysis, he was able to cite it himself. "I think it's unavoidable for any young actor to get into all this young-man paranoia, which is, 'Everybody wants to hurt me and *screw them.*' That's basically what's going on—'Screw Daddy' or something—so you gravitate toward roles that reinforce that feeling." One can easily see that psychological mechanism at work in Gere's own choices, as he played one rebel after another. His characters were sometimes out-and-out killers, such as the migrant worker in *Days of Heaven,* or the character he was soon to play in *Breathless,* a petty criminal who kills a policeman. Or they might merely be punks, like Tony Lopanto in *Looking for Mr. Goodbar* or Zack Mayo when he first arrives at OCS. Stony De Coco in *Bloodbrothers* was a rebel against parental authority, just as the "before" version of Zack Mayo was a rebel against the authority of the Navy. Julian Kay in *American Gigolo* was, at the very least, rebelling against the accepted order of relationships between men and women, and eventually he is punished by becoming a social outcast on the run from the law.

The only role Gere has played that lacked that "Screw Daddy" element of rebellion was Matt, the sweet, young American soldier in *Yanks*. Matt dutifully went off to fight for his country, and although he occasionally groused about the stupidity of the Army's rules, it certainly never occurred to him to rebel against them. It is interesting to remember that Gere said he prepared for the role of Matt by studying old photographs of his father; it seems in *Yanks* that he switched and quite literally identified himself *with* Daddy instead of with the forces undermining his authority. It will sooner or later be an important issue in Richard Gere's career: Can he be comfortable and convincing in roles that themselves incorporate some degree of authority? A whole generation of younger leading men—not only Gere but also De Niro, Pacino, Travolta, to name only the most obvious examples—seem to have their screen personas stuck in a stage of adolescent rebellion (whether or not they literally play adolescent characters). In *An Officer and a Gentleman*, Gere showed signs that he was ready to move beyond that stage and assume a persona that is, or becomes, part of the establishment. And the success of the film suggests that his fans might be ready to applaud the change.

Chapter Thirteen

Trying for Another Blockbuster

Richard Gere thought he had found the perfect movie to star in next: a remake of the 1960 classic French film *Breathless*. It seemed to have everything: a script that combined memorable lines from the original with the latest slang of the eighties, lots of sexy scenes of the sort no other male star could do so well, a fast-moving plot, a torrid romance, an ending to make audiences weep, wonderful cars, and the music of Jerry Lee Lewis to keep it all rolling. How could such a vehicle fail?

In fact, the movie very nearly didn't get made at all. The idea of a modern version of *Breathless* came to filmmaker Jim McBride and his writing partner, Kit Carson, over the summer of 1978. Carson explained why: "It broke my heart when I first saw it. . . . It was also the first picture that broke all sorts of rules and left you feeling that there were other ways to make a movie." They worked up a ten-page treatment and took it to independent producer Marty Erlichman (the man who "discovered" Barbra Streisand), who then had a multimovie deal going with Paramount. Studio execs there expressed tentative interest, so McBride and Carson set to work.

By Thanksgiving, they had created a script and also secured the rights to the remake from the director of the original film, Jean Luc Godard. According to Carson, "From the very beginning when we started writing the script, we heard that Richard Gere was interested in the film, but we were never brought together." Paramount seemed to favor Gary Busey, the frenetic star of *The Buddy Holly Story*, for the leading role. But when the script came in, most of the Paramount people lost interest; they would consider the project only if they could hire new writers. Erlichman, McBride, and Carson then went to Universal, where the production chief decided *he* was interested only if Carson dropped out and McBride agreed to let someone else do all the writing. In order to save the project they believed in, both men agreed. So another script was produced, and Universal sent it to Robert De Niro. When he turned it down, Universal dropped it.

Trying for Another Blockbuster

In early 1980, Orion expressed possible interest in the project, but they, too, became discouraged after both John Travolta and Al Pacino turned down the lead. They concluded the reason was McBride's relative inexperience as a director, so they issued an ultimatum: The project could only continue if McBride was willing to remove himself from it entirely. In early 1981, he agreed. Under this new condition, Paramount's early interest revived. They lined up Franc Roddam, who had directed *Quadrophenia*, to take over. He was interested, but he had a very definite idea about whom he wanted as his star—Richard Gere.

Gere was interested as soon as he read the McBride-Carson script, but events were not slated to work out so easily. With a director and star in place, the head of Paramount suddenly decided that he didn't want to make a movie about a cop-killer. So Roddam was given another assignment, but Richard Gere remained committed to *Breathless*. He decided to take the project under his own wing and turn it into a reality. And by that time, he had the Star Power to achieve his goal.

Gere went back to Orion and told them he wanted to do the film. That set in motion a hunt for a new director. Michael Mann was hired, and his first job was to write a new script. Everybody hated it. By this time, it was the spring of 1982, and at last someone at Orion

had the brilliant idea of asking the two origina-
tors of the project to return. Gere was initially
reluctant to have McBride direct, since he
had never handled a major production of this
size. But as he and McBride talked about
Breathless, Gere began to understand the validity of McBride's vision of the film. "You're the
first guy I've talked to who really understands
this movie," he told McBride. The director
laughed. "I ought to," he replied. "It was my
idea." Finally Gere agreed to go with McBride.

With the star and director signed, and the
studio giving the project enthusiastic support,
all that was needed was to produce the final
script. Gere wanted to be part of that process,
because he thought he could make a real contribution to the development of the hero's
character. Kit Carson later talked about the nature of the collaboration: "First meet-and-work
with Gere in my suite . . . It's been three years
since McBride and I have worked together, and
Gere is a stranger with squinty Roy Rogers eyes
and a certain cocky loneliness. But our guards
drop fast because there's just no time . . . So a
dynamic starts clicking around our triangle semi-
quickly. McBride and I take on our writing
partnership's roles: I'm the jerk at the type-
writer improving, overdoing lots of screwball
ideas; he's the skeptic who selects and modi-
fies the right ones. Gere clocks this game, and
the fun of it; he jumps in, sometimes taking my

side, sometimes Jim's, playing both the joker and the judge. An ironic, mocking ease develops among us."

The assignment facing this writing trio was a tough one: they were attempting to recreate a powerful and cherished original. *A Bout de Soufflé* was based on a brief story outline by François Truffaut. It was the tale of a petty gangster (Jean-Paul Belmondo) with a nihilistic attitude, who falls in love with an equally cool American girl (Jean Seberg). For both of them, this uncharacteristic emotion turns out to be fatally destructive. But any plot summary would be merely misleading; Godard's film was memorable not so much for its story as for its contemporary attitude—characters who don't seem to give a damn—and its startling cinematic techniques. The use of jump-cuts, hand-held cameras, and street locations gave it a look that harked back to the past of the movies and at the same time seemed very avant-garde.

But of course Godard's filmmaking innovations are now standard effects, and the attitude that surprised audiences in 1960 had become a cliché of contemporary civilization. So a remake would have to rely on similarity of plot and then create some sort of equivalent of the innovations. The writers agreed to begin with a focus on the similarities between their audiences and Godard's. Kit Carson explained: "When we wrote the script, we felt that this generation of kids are coming to the same sort of feelings that prompted Godard to make his film—the feeling of the future being very unclear. It's another lost generation, a generation that has no way to communicate with society." They concluded that, like the original, their film would be about extremes. And where better to set such a film than Los Angeles? Said Carson, "L.A. is on the edge. It's at the end of America, the last place, the extreme. It has extreme people, extreme buildings, extreme cars." In fact, Los Angeles came to be almost like a character in the film, and one of the most innovative aspects of the new *Breathless* was its use of what is generally thought of as "background." The set designer, Richard Sylbert, pointed out, "The film was written with the idea of the city as a billboard of itself, people's impressions of what they are, their playing roles and acting out their fantasies." Carson concluded that the city itself was "a compilation of contradictory elements that express a state of mind."

The plot they devised to be played out against the city was a paraphrase of the original. It tells the story of Jesse Lujack, a professional car thief who in a moment of panic shoots (and later discovers he has killed) a pursuing policeman. He holes up in Los Angeles with a French graduate student, Monica, whom he had met only a few days earlier. At first, she rejects him, distrusting his habit of living only for the present. But eventually she falls in love with his exuberance and vitality, and she agrees to run away with him to Mexico. But before they even get out of the Los Angeles city limits, she has second thoughts about the kind of future she would be letting herself in for. She concludes that the only way to induce him to run for safety without her is to call and turn him in to the cops, then tell him what she has done in time for him to leave immediately. But her plan misfires, and Jesse uses the precious minutes during which he should be escaping to try to find out whether Monica still loves him. The police arrive in time to catch him, and the film ends with a freeze-frame that shows Jesse making the move for his gun that will cause the police to start shooting, as Monica belatedly shouts, "I love you."

One of the strengths of the film is the complexity of the character of Jesse, and a lot of the credit for that goes to Richard Gere. Both as a writer and as an actor, he understood how to make Jesse three-dimensional and also attractive despite his obvious shortcomings. Carson described him as "this character who has shown up before. He was what Brando was in *On the Waterfront* and what Travolta was in *Saturday Night Fever*. He's sort of a good-hearted bad guy—but lovable." Gere himself affectionately called Jesse a "bozo," but stressed the fact that "this guy likes being on earth, which I think is different for a modern protagonist. He likes being here." Gere's hero is neither cool nor alienated, like Belmondo's; he is energetic, passionate, happy in a dopey sort of way, incapable of planning or foresight.

Carson told the press that the role of Jesse "allows Richard Gere to be touching, more open and more vulnerable than any other role he has had before." In an article for *Film Comment*, he wrote about the amazing experience of watching Richard Gere get into the character of Jesse. "This overheated afternoon, in a cramped Zoetrope office, Gere closes the gap between himself and the role, Jesse Lujack. For the last two months, we've been talking about Jesse: He's a 'gut-player, guy always doubles his bets when he's losing'; he's 'permanently running the edge, stuck at 180 mph'; etc. Okay, but this is just *talking* about a fiction. Soon now Gere's got to take the risk, make this wacko real. And abruptly this afternoon it seems to hit him in midsentence—we're reworking a scene, Gere's running Jesse's lines; and the words start going faster and faster, no pauses for breath, in a new erratic rhythm. I look over and he's standing up sweat-soaked behind the desk reading, laughing, snapping his shoulders, raving on, wide open. Sounds strange, but I watch Gere change himself: loosen the outline of his body, shake up his dimensions inside. Right then he gets it, or somehow Jesse Lujack taps into Richard Gere."

In addition to working on the script and approving the choice of a director, Richard Gere was also involved in casting the part of his leading lady. Early in the project, everyone agreed that Monica should be played by a French actress, preferably one unknown to American audiences. Gere and McBride flew to Paris and auditioned more than sixty attractive young actresses, using one of the love scenes between Jesse and Monica to check for the right chemistry between the stars. According to one account, that meant that Richard Gere spent three days in a hotel room, mostly naked, with a succession of passionate women. His comment on the experience: "I like women, but I tell you, after that I didn't care if I never saw a woman again."

The actress who finally won the role was nineteen-year-old Valerie Kaprisky. Before the final decision, she flew to Los Angeles for a five-minute screen test, which is referred to by the Hollywood insiders who have seen it as "Body Heat Plus." Here is one viewer's report: "They lie on a bed naked and glistening with sweat. As they speak, Gere slowly and noisily starts kissing his way up her body, beginning at her lap." Although Kaprisky was required to perform nude, Gere did it voluntarily, to make her feel more comfortable . . . how thoughtful. Kaprisky later spoke about her own feelings during that episode. "I didn't want to leave. I can't act without feelings and I felt something very special for Richard during that scene, and I didn't want to leave. In life, when you feel something for someone, you spend some time with them—not just ten minutes, some laughs and some tears, and then good-bye."

Throughout the entire filming of *Breathless*, it was difficult for Valerie Kaprisky to separate Richard Gere the actor from Jesse Lujack the character (and who knows, perhaps he had the same problem). She told a publicist, "It's not difficult to fall in love with a guy like Jesse. You feel like loving him because he's very alive. There are so many people now who just think about eating and surviving. But Jesse's alive. It's as if he's always running, moving, laughing, crying, shouting, screaming—doing something. And he makes her very sensual, much more than she thought she could be. Richard is not far from Jesse." When the shooting was over and she had to return to Paris, she wept over the separation. "It was wonderful working with Richard. He gives you everything to react to. We were not acting the love scenes. They were half real. You can't say you act only when they say 'Action!' " She concluded sadly, "People told me that friendships made when making a movie end. Without paying attention, I opened my heart too much and when I tried to close it, it wouldn't."

Trying for Another Blockbuster

This slight confusion of reality and make-believe may be one of the reasons that the love scenes in the film seem so relaxed and natural. Although there are some steamy moments, the most convincing aspect of the lovers' relationship is their unselfconsciousness about both their nudity and their sexuality. Richard Gere explained, "The characters are not coy about their bodies. In a way, it takes the voyeur aspect out of it, having them just walk around the way they do."

He is right on that point, but he has skipped over the hard part, which is how the actors manage to play the characters that way. Try to imagine what it must be like; think of yourself and one of your own colleagues at work: You're both nude, but you are surrounded by the rest of the people you work with, who are all fully clothed and watching every move you make . . . and the whir of a camera reminds you that eventually millions of people will have a chance to see . . . and you are attempting to simulate passionate lovemaking and to convince everyone that you are actually all alone in a bedroom and that you have been lovers before and will be again . . . now do you see how hard it is? Someone once asked Richard Gere if he got aroused during those passionate love scenes of which he is such a master, and he answered, "What? With fifty people standing around and all those lights?" But the point is, he can make it look as if he is aroused. That, dear fans, is called *acting*.

The director of *Breathless*, Jim McBride, was loud in his praise of Richard Gere as an actor and as a professional in the world of filmmaking. "Working with Richard has been a tremendously rewarding experience. He gives freely and unselfishly and professionally of himself and his talent, and he has contributed his whole being to this production." Writer Carson echoed, "It was a great experience." And co-star Kaprisky added, "He *feels* everything that he does. Richard is natural, sincere, spontaneous. . . ."

As usual, Richard Gere worked long, hard hours on the production without the slightest sign of any Star Temperament; he may sometimes be difficult with reporters and fans, but never with his professional colleagues. McBride commented on the fact that although he and Gere sometimes argued over the way scenes should be shot, Gere never once tried to use his leverage as a star to win the argument, but always dealt with it as a difference of opinion between professional equals. The rapport among the principals was so great that the shooting was accomplished in just eight weeks. When you consider how much of the film was shot on location—Westwood, the UCLA campus, Venice Beach, Beverly Hills, the Bonaventure Hotel in downtown L.A., the old Huntington mansion—you realize this is an amazingly short shoot for a major motion picture. Those weeks of work are rumored to have increased Gere's bank account by something in the vicinity of $1 million.

Breathless was released in May of 1983, amid a great wave of publicity. There were feature articles in magazines, analyses in serious film journals, and even a glorious picture of Richard Gere on the cover of *Newsweek*. But when the reviews started to appear, it was clear that critical opinion was mixed. Some of the negative reaction was almost surely due to the fact that the film invited—no, *demanded*—comparison with the original classic but was clearly unable to match its qualities of innovation and surprise. As *The New York Time*'s Vincent Canby said of the very idea of trying to remake the Godard film, "It's a little like trying to reinvent the light bulb to pay homage to Thomas Alva Edison. It can't easily be done, and the new *Breathless*, which is entertaining in its own way, carries a very heavy burden of built-in doubt." Not only did the film fail to live up to the standards of its predecessor, it also fell short of its own publicity. Billed as "a compelling drama of two people's obsessive and impassioned attraction for each other—a bond so strong that it breaks all the rules of society and the heart," the film was bound to disappoint, because the love story never managed to create that degree of power.

But *Breathless* was successful in its own way, first and foremost for Richard Gere's persuasive character study of Jesse Lujack. *Newsweek* said, "For Gere, the movie is a real advance. He takes more chances than he has before, and he hits new notes. What has often appeared as narcissistic posing is here incorporated into his character—and played for comic effect. He's playing a man who thinks he's cool, but isn't. Jesse's a hunk goofus who hands over this heart on a platter and is too much in love to protest when it gets broken." Vincent Canby was also impressed by the performance: "Mr. Gere plays Jesse Lujack with an uninhibited, lunatic energy that frequently comes close to parody, but it also gives the film a nutty nervous quality that fits." *People*, however, disagreed. "While Gere perfectly captures the jazzy, pretty-boy surface of his amoral character, he can't seem to cut deeper. Gere is not a bad actor, merely a limited one. Belmondo had reserves of talent to draw the audience in; Gere is not as well endowed."

Many of the reviews concentrated on other kinds of endowment. Pre-release publicity leaned heavily on the steaminess—and nudity—of the sex scenes so it is hardly surprising that much of what was written about *Breathless* was similarly skewed. *Variety* commented, "Gere's status as a sex star is certainly reaffirmed here, and not only does he appear with his shirt off through much of the pic, but he does some full-frontal scenes highly unusual for a major actor." *People* remarked that Kaprisky "plays her nude scenes with Gere as if the cameraman had gone home."

Naturally, all the focus of Gere's sexiness brought its own backlash. *New York*'s David Denby most forcefully stated the case for the prosecution: "Belmondo's Michel didn't know he was sexy, which is one of the reasons he *was* sexy. Richard Gere's Jesse, on the other hand, hardly knows anything else. In scene after scene, Gere goes through his hip-thrusting love-me routines, and since he also makes Jesse anxious and narcissistic, it's hard to enjoy him even as a purely sexual *image*. Gere does the kind of moves that Steve Martin and Dan Aykroyd were parodying only a few years ago. . . ." Denby did go on to say, "He has a few seconds, standing there naked, when his physical beauty and his self-destructive desire for the girl make him the sexual hero-outlaw that he's supposed to be," but then concluded unkindly, "You see too much of Richard Gere in *Breathless*, and I don't mean physically. His *soul* is immodest."

All the sex-oriented publicity probably did Richard Gere a disservice. Not only did it restrict him to the category of sex symbol, but also it kept some viewers from noticing the artistry of his performance. He is wonderfully convincing as Jesse, getting so far inside the part that even his co-star was fooled into thinking he was just "being himself." But of course, he wasn't; he was being Jesse, an artistic creation. The best part of *Breathless* is simply watching Jesse exist.

In box-office terms, *Breathless* fell short of being another *An Officer and a Gentleman*. But it's been the second most successful Gere film, and by the end of the summer was still hanging on to a respectable tenth place in the listing of box-office grosses. It will surely make money for Orion, and it emphasizes the fact that even when a Gere film fails to strike a nerve, it still draws good crowds. *Breathless* may not have increased Gere's stature in the movie business, but it didn't erode it, which is more than many stars can say about the film that follows a huge success. The future is still there, for Gere to make of it what he wants.

Chapter Fourteen

Coming Attractions

Richard Gere continues to display a serious lack of interest in vacations. He does his best to line up one project after another, allowing only the most minimal time in between. Part of the reason for such a tight schedule may be a very hard-boiled realism. He understands that although acting talent may be permanent, movie stardom is always cyclical. This year's hero may turn into next season's nobody, and fame can't be hoarded but rather must be spent in order to keep it. So Gere is using his Star Power while he has it, knowing full well that it may not last. Moreover, it is the very nature of the movie business that many films announced with a big flourish never actually get made. Gere has already experienced his share of such disappointments: projects that died for lack of studio support or had to be dropped when a director or co-star was suddenly unavailable. So he has learned that if he wants to be sure of keeping busy, he should be involved in more projects than he can actually manage to appear in, just to guarantee that something will be ready to go when he is.

And perhaps some of Richard Gere's seeming hyperactivity is also due to a degree of lingering inner tension. His friends do agree that he is more relaxed these days, and he himself thinks he is more mature. He says, "In a funny way, I think I'm also more childlike, less judgmental, less afraid." When novelist Richard Price visited Gere during the shooting of *Breathless*, he was impressed by the change. "He seemed like a different person—softer, easier. He'd lost that look of someone who's got World War III going on inside his head. He seemed more aligned." But it's hard to imagine Richard Gere ever being really laid back, and a certain amount of tension seems to be a chronic condition. Another exchange with Price makes this clear. When Price asked him if he was at that time the happiest he'd ever been, Gere answered, "Let's put it this way: I'm the farthest from suicide I've ever been." Then he laughed at the way his pronouncement sounded, but the statement was indicative. It's not easy for Richard Gere to relax and call himself happy.

Coming Attractions

While Richard Gere enjoys the status of Superstar, rumors fly thick and fast about his future; in particular, there is constant speculation over his future acting assignments (some of it fanned by optimistic producers and directors for whom the wish is father to the deed). It was reported that he was going to make a movie called *Marco*, about which nothing has ever been heard again. He was supposedly going to star opposite Elizabeth Taylor in Tennessee Williams's play, *Sweet Bird of Youth*; then we heard he'd been replaced by Treat Williams; now it seems doubtful that *anyone* is going to star with Liz in that particular vehicle. Michael Eisner, production chief at Paramount, says that Gere wants to star in a movie version of *Ethan Frome*, Edith Wharton's tragic novel about a romantic triangle on a remote New England farm. And although the interview with Eisner seemed to raise doubts that anyone at Paramount had ever actually read *Ethan Frome*, that is a mere detail. Observers believe that when Gere is ready to make the film, Paramount will back it. At one point, he seemed slated to star in a remake of the early Hitchcock thriller, *The Thirty-nine Steps*, but that project, too, has been moved to the back burner. He would still like to make a film with Antonioni, perhaps also Bertolucci; and the idea of making a screen version of *Bent* also still appeals to him.

Of course, not all the speculation about Gere's future projects is quite so serious. According to a humorous column in the new magazine *The Movies*, "The word in Hollywood is that Gere won't even read a script anymore unless he's assured that it contains a fat part for his bare buttocks." The writer went on to speculate that his future films might be remakes of *Moon over Miami*, *The Moon is Down*, *The Moon and Sixpence*, *The Moon is Blue*. Gere himself can be pretty funny on this subject. He told a reporter from Australia, in a deadpan way, "I have a clause in all my contracts that I have to do a nude scene," and then cracked up. He went on to add a more serious explanation: "To be honest, I don't know why a nude scene should be any more difficult than a scene where you are dredging up all of your fears and emotions. I'm not doing it because I want everyone to look at me. There's a reason for it, a reason to have it in the film. There's a reason for it to look right. That takes the narcissism and the self-consciousness out of it."

Gossip columns specialize in a different kind of rumor and try to connect all of his future films to new developments in his personal life. For example, there are currently stories afloat that he plans to make a film with Barbra Streisand, because there are also stories afloat that he is seeing her privately, in what has been called "a round of discreet dinners." It has also been reported that he plans to do a film with Susan Sarandon, who is supposedly his latest flame. Such gossip about a major star is inevitable, and although there is always the faint possibility that there might be a grain of truth in some of these stories, you shouldn't hold your breath waiting for these films to be released!

Out of this cloud of gossip and rumor, a few certainties do emerge. Richard Gere has, in fact, finished shooting his next film, which is scheduled for release in the fall of 1983. He began working on it just three days after he finished shooting *Breathless*, thereby once again successfully avoiding the threat of a vacation.

The new film is called *Beyond the Limit*, and it is based on *The Honorary Consul*, a novel by Graham Greene. Five years ago Norma Heyman, a former actress turned film executive, read the book and decided she wanted to create a screen version. After a long struggle, she finally found both the financial backing and the right talent to make the film. In the U.S., it is being released by Paramount.

Beyond the Limit is the story of a daring plan by guerrillas in a nameless South American province to kidnap an important English official. But the plot goes awry and instead they abduct an Englishman whose job is devoid of importance. The part of the "Honorary Consul" is played by Michael Caine. He commented, "It was a real departure for me. I've always played strong, young men—now I was playing an older, weaker one. But it's a very funny part as well, and in the end—like a lot of weak men—they look weak until they're under pressure and then the one you thought was going to collapse stands up to it marvelously."

Richard Gere plays the half-English doctor, Eduardo Plarr, who is slowly drawn into the kidnapping plot. Producer Heyman had seen him in *Bent* and offered him the role, which he accepted after he read the script by Christopher Hampton, based on the Greene novel. Plarr is involved both in the kidnapping and in a romantic triangle with the consul's beautiful young wife, whom he had found in a local brothel. Pre-release publicity suggests that once again there will be some steamy love scenes for Gere, playing opposite a young, unknown Mexican actress, Elpidia Carrillo.

Beyond the Limit was shot on location in three cities in Mexico: Veracruz, Coatzacoalcos farther south, and Mexico City. The director was John Mackenzie, a Scot whose best-known previous film was *The Long Good Friday*, about gang warfare in London. Mackenzie cast one of the stars of that film, Bob Hoskins, as the local police chief who must deal with the kidnapping, and was also responsible for selecting Elpidia Carrillo from over two hundred actresses who auditioned for the chance to play opposite Gere and Caine.

All in all, the role of Eduardo Plarr seems very much in the usual mold of Richard Gere roles. His dark good looks have already led to his casting as an "ethnic" type, so playing a half-Latin hero is no departure. Moreover, the character is another rebel against the accepted order, which is how he is usually cast. And the character is involved in a romantic relationship, as has been the case with every Gere movie except *Bloodbrothers*. He has commented, "If every movie I've done has had relationships with women in it, why not? Relationships are important to me in my life. They seem important to everybody else's life, too."

With *Beyond the Limit* in the can, Richard Gere returned to New York. By the summer of 1983, he had embarked on his next project, a film called *Cotton Club*. It is about the legendary Harlem nightclub, which attracted the best of the jazz performers and the most enthusiastic of the fans during its heyday in the twenties and thirties. Richard Gere plays a former trumpet player who gives up performing and turns instead to running the nightclub. There will be sequences in the film that utilize Gere's real-life musical talents, and he spent some preparation time practicing the trumpet, piano and guitar so he would be ready.

The film, an Orion release, is being produced

by Robert Evans. The director will be Francis Ford Coppola, who has also written the final script, reworking an earlier draft by Mario Puzo. If you can believe what you read in the trades, Coppola is being paid $3 million for directing, plus a hefty fee for his writing work, and Richard Gere's salary is in excess of $2 million. (For *Beyond the Limit*, he was reportedly paid a mere $1.6 million.) Both Coppola and Gere also have a profit participation in the picture, but as many of Hollywood's famous stars have discovered ruefully (in some celebrated cases the reaction has been *sue* instead of *rue*), a profit participation may mean nothing at all unless it comes out of the gross rather than the net. Films that do quite well at the box office may have so many expenses charged against them that there is never a net profit. For example, according to top movie auditor Phil Hacker, Gere's *American Gigolo* has grossed $24,066,100, but the books show a current net profit of − $925,500,—which means that Richard Gere has yet to see a cent beyond his salary.

Cotton Club is obviously slated to be a big picture. In addition to Gere, it will star Gregory Hines, the Broadway musical star, and the leading lady will be Diane Lane. She appeared in the last Coppola film, *The Outsiders*, playing opposite the youthful Matt Dillon. The failure of that movie did nothing for her career, but Coppola continues to have faith in this talented young actress. (Newspaper stories refer to her as his "protegée," whatever that may mean.) The movie is being shot on location in New York, and the studio work will take place at the new Astoria Studios in Queens. Presumably, *Cotton Club* will be released sometime in 1984.

And don't worry, fans, there will be another film after that. Paramount Pictures has recently announced that Richard Gere will star in *The Story of David*, which will go into production in early 1984. It is a Biblical epic, the first of that genre to be made in a long time and will follow the story of David from his early life as an innocent shepherd through his reign as the first great King of Judah.

Richard Gere will, of course, play David, and one assumes that there will be a torrid love story in the film; you remember all that in the Bible about David and Bathsheba. The director will be Australian Bruce Beresford, whose previous credits include *Tender Mercies, Puberty Blues*, and the international hit, *Breaker Morant*. Beresford and producer Martin Elfand have already scouted suitable locations in Italy for the filming, and Andrew Birkin has completed the screenplay.

It seems clear from what we know of those forthcoming films that Richard Gere continues to search for new challenges, to be unafraid of risk. He told an interviewer recently, "I don't see any reason for playing the same part again.

There's no point. I suppose I act, every time, to find out things, new things. I certainly don't want to have the same impulses as a man or as an actor that I had at twenty years of age when I'm fifty." And he *would* like to escape from the restrictions of being thought of simply as a sex symbol. He is more philosophical about that problem today than he used to be, but for a serious actor, it must be annoying to have so many reviews concentrate on physical dimensions rather than emotional ones.

Chapter Fifteen

An Enduring Screen Image

Richard Gere is unarguably one of the foremost male stars of his generation.

What is the secret of his appeal? The answer to this question is undoubtedly to be found on the screen, rather than in the actor's personal life. There are stars who appeal to us largely because of what we know—or think we know—about their offscreen activities. The best current example is Elizabeth Taylor, with her many husbands and her dramatic illnesses, her jewel-bedecked weight problem, her never-ending search for true love and happiness. Raising the question of whether or not she is a good actress is quite irrelevant: it's Miz Liz the Star who captivates the public imagination rather than Cleopatra, or Maggie the Cat, or Martha who's afraid of Virginia Woolf. To a certain extent, the same is true of many of Hollywood's most popular leading men. We follow Warren Beatty's much-publicized romances, Paul Newman's racing career and promotion on behalf of his salad dressing, and Robert Redford's support of environmental causes.

Bur Richard Gere has resolutely refused to play the publicity game of using his personal life as a way of attracting attention and fame. He insists on keeping his private life genuinely private. As he put it, "I don't want to be a personality. How can anyone pay attention to Elizabeth Taylor's work when they know all about her six or seven husbands? I don't want to be invaded. If I just wanted to be in the public eye, I'd climb the Empire State Building. It would be a lot easier. . . ." So Richard Gere maintains a low profile. He is rarely photographed attending openings, dating starlets, making the Hollywood scene. He still won't appear on television even to promote his latest movie, let alone to promote himself. He is reluctant to grant interviews, and he doesn't release personal publicity photos. (If you look carefully at most magazine articles about Gere, you will begin to notice that they are illustrated with stills from his recent movies rather than candid photos of his private life.) We don't know whether he has a dog, what his favorite color is, or if he likes to sleep in the nude . . . all great unanswered questions of our time.

However, this determination to remain a private person doesn't mean he lives like a recluse. In New York, he eats out a lot, mostly at casual restaurants in the Village, such as Texarkana. He goes to rock concerts (he's a fan of Elvis Costello and Randy Newman). And he maintains a down-to-earth lifestyle that involves doing a lot of his own errands rather than depending on an entourage. But when he does decide to go out, he tries to act like one more face in the New York crowd, and thus he escapes both fans and photographers. And the public continues to learn very little about his private life.

In other words, even the most dedicated Richard Gere fans don't really know very much about him personally. They may daydream, but when it comes right down to it, what makes them fans is not the "real" Richard Gere, but the image they see on the screen. Each new role adds something to his screen persona, and it is the remembered moments from all those films—the residue—that create our idea of Richard Gere. We owe "our" Richard Gere to the work of screenwriters and directors; to his physical presence; and, most of all, to his artistic ability to bring to life in our minds the characters he plays.

For many fans, the main attraction of the

Richard Gere image is admittedly a sexual one. Let's face it, the man has a great body. And he is quite willing to display it to the audience whenever the action is natural for his character. Gere displays onscreen an erotic combination of hard muscle and smooth skin; he knows how to pose to make the most of both assets. He is also graceful when he moves, with a neat, surefooted walk that gives a hint of his athletic ability, and an admirable balance and posture. He always seems to be in complete control of his physical being, whether he is naked or clothed. And there are really very few other leading men who can compete with him on purely physical terms. It is interesting in this connection to note that John Travolta, with whom Gere has frequently been compared throughout their careers, has recently reworked his rather slight body to make it more like Gere's. Perhaps that's why he recently told a reporter that he thinks the three sexiest men in America are himself first, Sylvester Stallone second, and Richard Gere third.

No doubt Richard Gere's casual attitude toward baring some or all of that handsome body is one reason that his fans think he is so sexy. But as most adults have long since discovered, nudity alone isn't always enough to turn someone on; in fact, it may have just the opposite effect. In Richard Gere's case, it's not just the sight of his body, it's the way he uses it that leaves us a little short of breath. He has in the past been criticized for his posturing, his narcissism, the "love-me" demands implicit in the way he presents himself to the camera. It may be true that some of his earlier performances are marred by a degree of consciousness about his appeal; but as Gere has matured professionally, he has become more relaxed and much less likely to project the intention of making us admire him. Nowadays, his sexiness seems very natural and unforced. This was particularly evident in *Breathless*, where his onscreen nudity was amazingly unselfconscious.

Another reason Richard Gere seems so sexy is that he is a master of body language. You can prove this to yourself by checking out some of his photographs. He usually sits or stands in what experts call an "open" or inviting posture—arms at his sides, hands not blocking his body, his head and torso turned toward the camera and thus the viewer. His lower body is also open, with legs uncrossed, knees apart, feet forming a slight V. It's not obscene, but it is, shall we say, welcoming. Only in a few candid shots of Gere being himself, discussing a scene with the director or standing alone in front of the camera without the protection of a part to play, do we see the closed posture: arms folded over chest to shut people out, shoulders angled away from the viewer, eyes focused somewhere off in the middle distance. These are the times that he feels defensive or insists on holding some part of himself back. As long as he can be in character, Richard Gere's body seems to know instinctively how to speak to an audience to make him seem available.

However, the true secret of Richard Gere's screen appeal is much more complicated than his ability to project an alluring brand of sexual availability. His effect on audiences is not merely sexual, but emotional as well. His face, with its erotic eyes and full, sensual mouth, can change very suddenly and confront us with an entirely different person. Sometimes he looks very tough, and then we notice the high, menacing cheekbones, the squint of the eyes, the street fighter's nose, the near sneer of the mouth. At those moments he seems like a kid who grew up on the wrong side of the tracks and learned to battle for every single thing he wanted. The factory worker in *Days of Heaven* utilized this side of Gere, as did the role of Tony in *Looking for Mr. Goodbar*, and the character of the young Zack Mayo in *An Officer and a Gentleman*. Yet he can just as quickly turn vulnerable when the mouth curves into a touching boy's grin or when the eyes soften and Gere appears to be struggling to keep from bursting into tears. It is the vulnerable Gere we see in Matt in *Yanks*, and in Jesse Lujack when Monica refuses to go with him in *Breathless*, and in Julian Kay when he realizes in *American Gigolo* just how alone he is.

What is truly appealing about Richard Gere's screen image is the combination of all these elements: the erotic attraction, the tough exterior, and the hint of concealed vulnerability. Cathleen McGuigan, writing in *Newsweek*, said, "His appeal stems in part from an ability to project menace and vulnerability at the same time. In *Officer*, he looked like he might explode any minute; after a night of lovemaking with girl-friend Debra Winger, you felt he could reject all her motherly attentions and throw the eggs she's just scrambled back in her face." Some writers have compared this appeal to that generated by John Garfield, another tough-tender icon. Others suggest he is more similar to James Cagney in his projection of a sense of restrained violence tempered by personal vulnerability. (Critic Lincoln Kirsten once defined the basis of American male sex appeal as "the delights of violence, the overtones of a semiconscious sadism, the tendency toward destruction, toward anarchy. . . .") Male viewers like to indentify with the macho qualities of this image, and females like to believe that only with someone like them could such a man reveal his hidden tenderness.

But director Paul Schrader has analyzed Richard Gere's screen persona along slightly different lines. "He comes from a long line of strong, sensitive matinee idols, a lineage that has been impoverished of late. Paul Newman and Alain Delon are the outstanding examples. They project the sexuality of a star who's sensitive without being neurotic. Not to diminish De Niro or Pacino, but they are from a different tradition. Gere stands in one we've been a little short on lately. Richard fills a vacancy as Newman grows older." There are indications that Gere might not be flattered by at least some of these comparisons. One interviewer met him in a room that contained a poster of Alain Delon and Gere commented, "There was a time when I tried to pick up on his pouty narcissism. Look at his face. Don't you just want to slap him silly?"

Gere himself apparently prefers to put the emphasis on his ability to portray a kind of masculine strength and decisiveness, rather than his sensitivity. And this emphasis corresponds to something in the tenor of the times. The much-discussed current trend toward popularity of "hunks" with women audiences may be partly the result of a more open expression of female sexuality, but a more significant component is the desire to return to some earlier romantic vision of men as being decisive, dynamic, determined. Perhaps women who have gained their independence are even more likely than their male-dependent predecessors to daydream about a strong and virile man who will sweep them off their feet. The fact that in real life they insist on egalitarian relationships turns their fantasies toward dominant men who can magically relieve them of all the burdens of adulthood and independence. So a screen hero who weeps, vacillates, and agonizes over his feelings is not attractive to these women; nor is he to men, who fear the weakness of such a male role model, even when it reflects much of the reality of their own lives. Thus Jesse Lujack, who breaks into his girlfriend's apartment to wait for her, who won't take no for an answer, who insists on sweeping Monica away from her real life to become a part of his fantasy, and who finally prevails upon her to agree to it, is a movie hero for our times. It is obvious that a real-life Monica would reject Jesse's pleas to go to Mexico because it would put an end to the career in architecture she was working for; but watching Jesse on the screen provides an agreeable escapist fantasy that makes it a little easier to go back home and return to work on those drawings that have to be ready Monday morning.

When Richard Gere was younger, he seemed to take a certain interest in displaying his capacity for suffering and the delicacy of his tormented soul. Personally, he gave some moody interviews that contained comments like, "Anonymity is the only way you can be an outlaw," and, "The only real saints are unknown." Professionally, he let the camera linger over his brooding features in *Days of Heaven* and tried to show us the anguish of a sensitive young man trapped in a family where brutality is the norm in *Bloodbrothers*. But as he has matured, he has rejected that sort of romanticism and replaced it with a masculine willingness to take responsibility. That was the appeal of Matt in *Yanks*, of the matured Zack in *An Officer and a Gentleman*. It is even the appeal of Jesse in *Breathless*. Gere makes him not a tortured adolescent outlaw, but a cheerfully dumb loser who hustles forward to disaster under his own steam—a much more interesting and complex character, and one better calculated to appeal to modern audiences.

Added together, these and other moments create the image of Richard Gere that is cherished by his fans. And his new roles in films to come will add to that image, just as it adds to the total pleasure we've received by watching it. Richard Gere is too smart, too analytical, too self-aware to remain static; time, and his maturity, will give the image increased depth, added complexity—perhaps even unexpected surprises. The one thing we can be sure of is that it will continue to be interesting, provocative . . . and well worth watching.

Appendix

A Richard Gere Filmography

Report to the Commissioner
United Artists 1975
Producer: M. J. Frankovich
Director: Milton Katselas
Screenplay: Abby Mann and Ernest Tidyman,
    based on the novel by James Mills
Cinematography: Mario Tosi
Running time: 112 minutes
Cast: Michael Moriarty, Yaphet Kotto, Susan
    Blakely, Hector Elizonda, Tony King,
    Michael McGuire, Richard Gere in a bit
    part

Baby Blue Marine
Columbia Pictures 1976

Producers: Aaron Spelling and Leonard Goldberg
Director: John Hancock
Screenplay: Stanford Whitemore
Cinematography: Laszlo Kovacs
Running time: 89 minutes
Cast: Jan-Michael Vincent, Glynnis O'Connor,
Katherine Helmond, Dana Elgar, Bert
Remsen, B. Kirby, Jr., Richard Gere, Art
Lund, Michael Conrad, Michael LeClair,
Allan Miller

Looking for Mr. Goodbar
Paramount 1977
Producer: Freddie Fields
Director: Richard Brooks
Screenplay: Richard Brooks, based on the novel
by Judith Rossner
Cinematography: William A. Fraker
Running time: 136 minutes
Cast: Diane Keaton, Tuesday Weld, William
Atherton, Richard Kiley, Richard Gere,
Alan Feinstein, Tom Berenger, Priscilla
Palmer, Laurie Prande, Joel Fabiani,
Julius Harris, LeVar Burton

Days of Heaven
Paramount 1978
Producers: Bert and Harold Brackman
Director: Terence Malick
Screenplay: Terence Malick
Cinematography: Nestor Almendros

Running time: 92 minutes
Cast: Richard Gere, Brooke Adams, Sam Shepard,
    Linda Manz, Robert Wilke, Jackie Shultis,
    Stuart Margolin, Tim Scott, Gene Bell,
    Doug Kershaw

Bloodbrothers
Warner Brothers 1978
Producer: Stephan Friedman
Director: Robert Mulligan
Screenplay: Walter Newman, based on the novel
    by Richard Price
Cinematography: Robert Surtees
Running time: 116 minutes
Cast: Paul Sorvino, Tony Lo Bianco, Richard
    Gere, Lelia Goldoni, Yvonne Wilder,
    Kenneth McMillan, Floyd Levine, Marilu
    Henner, Michael Hershewe

Yanks
Universal 1979
Producers: Joseph Janni and Lester Persky
Director: John Schlesinger
Screenplay: Colin Welland and Walter Bernstein,
    based on a story by Welland
Cinematography: Dick Bush
Running time: 139 minutes
Cast: Richard Gere, Lisa Eichhorn, Vanessa
    Redgrave, William Devane, Chick Ven-
    ners, Wendy Morgan, Rachel Roberts,
    Tony Melody, Martin Smith

American Gigolo
Paramount 1980
Producer: Jerry Bruckheimer
Director: Paul Schrader
Screenplay: Paul Schrader
Cinematography: John Bailey
Running time: 117 minutes
Cast: Richard Gere, Lauren Hutton, Hector Elizondo, Nina Van Pallandt, Bill Duke, Brian Davies, K. Callen, Tom Stewart, MacDonald Carey in a small part

An Officer and a Gentleman
Paramount 1982
Producer: Martin Elfand
Director: Taylor Hackford
Screenplay: Douglas Day Stewart
Cinematography: Donald Thorin
Running time: 126 minutes
Cast: Richard Gere, Debra Winger, David Keith, Robert Loggia, Lisa Blount, Lisa Eilbacher, Louis Gossett, Jr, Tony Plana, Harold Sylvester, David Caruso

Breathless
Orion 1983
Producer: Martin Erlichman
Director: Jim McBride
Screenplay: Jim McBride and Kit Carson
Cinematography: Richard H. Kline
Running time: 105 minutes

Cast: Richard Gere, Valerie Kaprisky, William Tepper, John P. Ryan, Robert Dunn, Waldemar Kalinowski, Art Metrano, Gary Goodrow, Eugene Lourie

Beyond the Limit
World Film Services/Paramount Pictures 1983
Producer: Norma Heyman
Director: John Mackenzie
Screenplay: Christopher Hampton, based on the novel *The Honorary Consul* by Graham Greene
Cinematography: Phil Meheux
Cast: Michael Caine, Richard Gere, Elpidia Carrillo, Bob Hoskins, Joaquim de Almeida, A. Martinez, Stephanie Cotsirilos, Adriana Roel, Domingo Ambriz, Leonard Maguire

Cotton Club
Orion 1984
Producer: Robert Evans
Director: Francis Ford Coppola
Screenplay: Francis Ford Coppola, based on an early draft by Mario Puzo
Cast: Richard Gere, Gregory Hines, Diana Lane

The Story of David
Paramount late 1984 or early 1985
Producer: Martin Elfand

RICHARD GERE

Director: Bruce Beresford
Screenplay: Andrew Birkin
Cast: Richard Gere, the rest of the cast to be
    announced

More Biography and Autobiography from SIGNET

(0451)

☐ **BOB DYLAN by Anthony Scaduto with an Introduction by Steven Gaines.** (092899—$2.50)*

☐ **UP & DOWN WITH THE ROLLING STONES by Tony Sanchez.** (119339—$3.50)

☐ **SINATRA by Earl Wilson.** (074874—$2.25)

☐ **FONDA: MY LIFE as told to Howard Teichmann.** (118588—$3.95)*

☐ **BOGIE by Joe Hyams.** (091892—$1.75)

☐ **KATE: THE LIFE OF KATHERINE HEPBURN by Charles Higham.** (112121—$2.95)*

☐ **FIRST, YOU CRY by Betty Rollin.** (112598—$2.50)

☐ **IF YOU COULD SEE WHAT I HEAR by Tom Sullivan and Derek Gill.** (118111—$2.75)*

☐ **W.C. FIELDS: HIS FOLLIES AND FORTUNES by Robert Lewis Taylor.** (506537—$1.25)

*Prices slightly higher in Canada

Buy them at your local

bookstore or use coupon

on next page for ordering.

Quintessential Quiz Books from SIGNET

(0451)

☐ **THE ELVIS PRESLEY TRIVIA QUIZ BOOK by Helen Rosenbaum.**
(081781—$1.50)

☐ **THE SOAP OPERA TRIVIA QUIZ BOOK by Jason Bonderoff.**
(117506—$2.75)*

☐ **THE SOAP OPERA TRIVIA QUIZ BOOK #2 by Jason Bonderoff.**
(125193—$2.95)

☐ **THE ROLLING STONES TRIVIA QUIZ BOOK by Helen Rosenbaum.**
(086694—$1.75)

☐ **THE NOSTALGIA QUIZ BOOK by Martin A. Gross.**
(110358—$2.50)*

☐ **TREKKIE QUIZ BOOK by Bart Andrews.** (116569—$1.95)†

☐ **THE COUNTRY MUSIC TRIVIA QUIZ BOOK by Dennis Hazzard.**
(121414—$2.25)*

☐ **THE FIRST OFFICIAL NFL TRIVIA QUIZ BOOK by Ted Brock and Jim Campbell.** (095413—$1.95)

☐ **THE SECOND NFL TRIVIA QUIZ BOOK by Jim Campbell.**
(117891—$2.25)*

☐ **THE ULTIMATE BASEBALL QUIZ BOOK by Dom Forker.**
(096797—$2.50)*

☐ **THE ULTIMATE YANKEE BASEBALL QUIZ BOOK by Dom Forker.**
(114299—$2.95)*

☐ **THE ULTIMATE WORLD SERIES QUIZ BOOK by Dom Forker.**
(117883—$1.95)*

☐ **THE ULTIMATE PRO-BASKETBALL QUIZ BOOK by Dom Forker.**
(118421—$2.95)*

*Price slightly higher in Canada
†Not available in Canada
